SHADOW SHOW

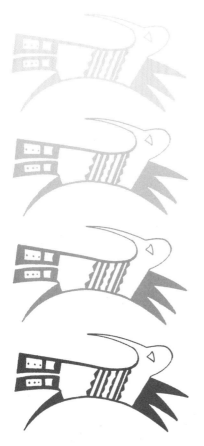

SHADOW SHOW
An Autobiographical Insinuation
JAMAKE HIGHWATER

ALFRED VAN DER MARCK EDITIONS • NEW YORK

Portions of this book appeared in substantially different form in *The Soho Weekly News*, *The New York Times*, *Saturday Review*, *The Chicago Tribune*, *The Los Angeles Free Press*, *Stereo Review*, *Jazz and Pop*, *Dance Magazine*, *Vogue*, *The New York Philharmonic Program*, and *Esquire*.

It was editorial director Robert Walter who originally proposed that I do a book composed of selections from the rather wide ranging and numerous articles and essays I have written over the last twenty years. The idea delighted me for a number of reasons. But it is only the shadow of a memoir, for it excludes so many of the significant events and important people of my life. That larger story I am saving as a project for the future.

Jamake Highwater
Connecticut, 1986

Editorial director: Robert Walter

Managing editor: Leonard Neufeld

Designer: Ellen Friedman

Typographers: Americomp, Brattleboro, Vermont

Photo of Jamake Highwater on the back of the dust jacket is by Johan Elbers.

Copyright © 1986 by Alfred van der Marck Editions.

Alfred van der Marck Editions
1133 Broadway, Suite 1301
New York, N.Y. 10010

Library of Congress Cataloging-in-Publication Data

   Highwater, Jamake.
     Shadow show.

     1. Highwater, Jamake—Biography.   2. Highwater, Jamake—Friends and associates.   3. Authors, American—20th century—Biography.   4. United States—Intellectual life—20th century.   I. Title.
PS3558.I373Z477   1986   818'.5409 {B}   85-40823
   ISBN 0-912383-24-0

First printing: November 1986

"... it was she who first gave me the idea that a person doesn't stand motionless and clear before us—with his merits, his defects, his plans, his intentions in regard to us exposed on the surface.... [Instead, he] is but a shadow, which we can never successfully penetrate, and of which we can never have direct knowledge, that allows us to form countless beliefs, based upon his words and sometimes upon his behavior, for words and actions can only give us inadequate and contradictory information.... [He is] a shadow behind which we can alternatively imagine, with equal justification, that there burns the flame of hatred and of love."

Marcel Proust

IN MEMORY OF RICHARD THURN
1942–1986

Soave sia il vento,
tranquilla sia l'onda,
ed ogni elemento benigno risponda
ai nostri desir!

Lorenzo da Ponte

C O N T E N T S

INTRODUCTION:
BORROWED LIVES

The final belief is to believe in a fiction, which you know to
be a fiction, there being nothing else, the exquisite truth is to
know that it is a fiction and that you believe in it willingly.
—Wallace Stevens, *Opus Posthumous*

I am a shadow . . . someone who was adopted as a child, at a time
when adoption was still a covert matter. The greatest mystery of my
life is my own identity. So I have always been fascinated by the efforts of people to construct a history out of the things they recall,
the things they think they remember but which may have been told

to them, and the fabrications and secrets insisted upon by many families.

Jean-Paul Sartre once said that we are the consummation of everything that has ever happened to us: all the people we have known and loved and loathed. We are our lives and nothing more.

In the process of becoming a writer, I have discovered something quite unexpected: that many authors who were not adopted and who possess a personal history are nonetheless obsessed with the need to construct a personal mythology that is larger than their lives. William Butler Yeats once said that art is the public act of a private person. But for many artists it is necessary for their lives to become an intrinsic part of their art and for their art to become part of their lives.

Joseph Campbell tells us that "it is a curious characteristic of our unformed species that we live and model our lives through acts of make-believe."

We are myth makers. We are legenders. Of all the animals we alone are capable of dreaming ourselves into existence. Such an activity is not devious. To the contrary, it represents the core of our capacity for scientific invention, philosophical inquiry, and the creation of masterworks of art. Yet in our current world this astounding ability to *imagine* is so rare that it has become unfamiliar and suspicious.

"The principle which interests me," says E. L. Doctorow, "is that reality isn't something outside. It's something we compose every moment."

Anais Nin once told me: "We write to create a world that is truer than the one before us."

The American painter Arthur Dove said much the same thing: "We cannot express the light in nature because we have not the sun. We can only express the light we have in ourselves."

Yet some people refuse to express the light within them. I am utterly confounded by such people.

As a boy I was very badly burned. I still have the faint scars, which were a source of great self-consciousness when I was an adolescent, but I cannot recall the fire. That day has vanished—the place, the flames, even the agony. A first principle of Buddhism is: *Pain exists.*

To escape things that are painful we must reinvent ourselves. Either we reinvent ourselves or we choose not to be anyone at all.

We must not feel guilty if we are among those who have managed to survive.

I begin to think that our borrowed lives are necessities in a world filled with hostility and pain, a confusing world largely devoid of credible social truths. We do not have the sun within us, and yet we must have a light so we can find our way through the darkness. Our imaginations illuminate and, finally, define our reality. The light by which we see is a mythic lantern. And the world it lights provides us with the only images by which we know ourselves and what we have been and what we are becoming. Imagination is a process that puts us in touch with the only truth left to us—that which flows from whatever it is within each of us that we call "myself."

AVEC LE TEMPS: ANAIS NIN

Avec le temps, va
Tout s'en va . . .
    —Leo Ferré

When word came from Los Angeles on January 14, 1977, that Anais Nin was gone, I angrily pushed aside the work in front of me and turned to a precious folio of letters from the past. Among them were letters containing the words of an exuberant woman who had befriended me almost from the first day I decided to be a writer. Though I have often heard tales of the competitive outbursts of

Dear J — Don't let what happens
to me discourage you. I have
many handicaps you don't have.
I'm a woman, and I have been
"typed" as avant garde. This is the
age of the young man writer — a good
moment for you. Have you tried
Discovery and New World Writing?
Do you have a agent? It is
absolutely essential to have an
agent. Publishers read last those
who are not introduced by an agent.
Rupert and I will try to have
dinner at Albatross one evening.
My case as a writer is individual.
You may have a much easier time.
But I would advise you to go to N.Y.
It is easier for a writer there —
Impossible in California unless
you work for the studios. N.Y.
is a writer's city. You could
meet an agent, magazine people etc
Don't lose courage. I haven't —

Anaïs

A letter from Anais Nin

Anais Nin, to me she was a voice of unfailing concern and persistent affection and generosity.

Anais had a sense about people. She had no patience with quitters and upstarts. She instantly knew which of us could be counted upon to fight things out to the end. Fortunately for me, she detected my tenacity, and so I became one of the young writers who received her encouragement, criticism, and advice.

Here is a letter she scribbled on a sheet of American Airlines stationery as she hovered over the American landscape en route from Los Angeles to New York, two cities in which she lived drastically different lives.

I was a terribly displaced kid, living in the San Fernando Valley with a foster family that claimed me as its own despite my confused recollections of another family, another home, another history. Even my name had been changed. For many years I would be known as "J. Marks."

I trailed after my foster father, who was in the motion picture business, first terrified, then awed, and finally dismayed by him. He insisted upon my playing the role of his son. So I trudged after him and his friends as they daily played thirty-six holes of golf, and I lagged behind when he took me to the studio, hoping to rouse in me the illusion that I might one day be a movie star. John Michael-john at Paramount Pictures put all such family ambition to rest when he gazed momentarily at me with brows incredulously raised and pronounced judgment: "I can tell you one thing, he'll never be a leading man." (I was not an attractive child.) But my family did not give up: I suffered through dancing, singing, and acting lessons, and even mock religious rites that failed to exorcise the barbarian in me. I frustrated every plan my foster father made for my life, until he finally abandoned me to the classical music he hated and to my ever-clattering typewriter.

I had decided to be a writer, despite the fact that I could barely read or write and was horrendously self-conscious and inarticulate. While other children filled their days with friends and outings, I sat at an old typewriter in our home in the then-rural Valley and spent my childhood trying to release the cry of rage that was buried within me. I abandoned the past and started to fill page after page with misshapen prose and poetry, until at last I found the door that opened between the person trapped inside of me and the outer world in which I felt utterly alien. Finally the words began to flow in a swift and endless current and in a voice I hardly recognized.

Anais Nin read what I had written and decided that I might have whatever it takes to make a writer. She was the first person to whom I showed my work. I waited fearfully for five weeks for her response. And when she said that there was in my short story something that vaguely reminded her of Virginia Woolf—some echo of dread and remorse—I wept. Her criticism and encouragement became a lifeline that kept me afloat above the flood of my own uncertainty. Even now as I search for the place in my mind where the words create themselves, I often think of Anais.

I had met Anais Nin through James Leo Herlihy. In those days—around 1950—he worked at a bookshop in Hollywood where I spent hours among the stacks of ragged literary magazines and old novels. Slowly and with great difficulty, I was learning how to read, and books—just the smell and feel of them—had become objects of immense fascination. I was intrigued and frightened by the crowd of words that filled the pages, by the shear magnitude of the effort that writers expended upon their creations. Herlihy must have grasped both my alienation and my bitter need for friends. Though I didn't realize it at the time, he was extremely good-looking. Later, people sometimes commented on his vanity, but I always regarded such remarks as envious. Jamie wore his marvelous looks with the inward assurance of a fine, thoroughbred creature that stands far beyond the reach of envy.

Though I was youthful—still in my early teens—and rather stupid and had utterly nothing to offer him, he encouraged my interest in books. He suggested writers I should read: William Faulkner, Frederick Buechner, Jack Dunphy, William Goyen, Paul Bowles, and T. S. Eliot. He talked to me about his own aspirations of becoming a great writer, of quitting his job at the bookstore and going off to *New York!* (The very name of that city delighted us.) He told me about a marvelous woman he had met named Anais Nin. She had become his friend, reading his stories and introducing him to the eccentric art community of Southern California. Sometimes Jamie

James Leo Herlihy

showed me the things he was writing: stories full of strange people and fierce landscapes.

Then one afternoon he burst into the bookstore and told me that he had published a short story, a piece called "Laughter in the Graveyard." I felt so great a surge of pleasure from the news that I couldn't speak. It seemed almost unthinkable that someone I personally knew was actually going to have a short story published. Writing had always been something of a fantasy to me. So Jamie's success suddenly turned that fantasy into an unexpected reality.

Literature was crucial to my existence. I became truly obsessed with writers. I began to find power in writing. That sense of power gave me a new courage to communicate with people by letter. And so I began to write to the novelists and poets I most cherished. When I look back on the audacity of my childhood correspondence I am both amused and amazed—amused by my capacity to convey the impression that I was an adult and amazed that I inevitably received responses to my letters. Frederick Buechner wrote to me at length about his first novel, *A Long Day's Dying*. Archibald MacLeish filled his letter to me with remarkable insights into the nature of poetry and metaphor.

And then one day in early June of 1951, a letter on the stationery of Faber and Faber Publishers of London arrived, signed by a poet whose influence upon me was immense:

Dear Mr. Marks,

Thank you for your kind letter of May 29th. I appreciate your writing as you have done, and asking for my permission {to dedicate your novel to me}, and I do not see any reason why you should not dedicate the book to myself. I should only be obliged if you would first let me see the form of dedication which you propose, as I like only a small dedication, without any expanse of compliment.

Yours sincerely,

T. S. Eliot

(The childhood novel dedicated to Eliot, along with six other novels and several years of journals, vanished in a ceremonial fire long ago.)

The friendliness of great writers was essential both to my development as a writer and to my acquisition of the courage it takes to

write. But these writers were widely separated from my rural world
in the San Fernando Valley. Only Anais Nin seemed real to me.
Then in February of 1954, Anais left for New York, and I told Jim
Herlihy that I didn't think I could survive without her. I spilled out
my melodramatic despair in a long letter to Anais. I was a youngster
and I didn't realize that at the time she was ill and worried and very
busy. Yet she put aside whatever she was doing and wrote a letter
to me which has always been a precious source of power. And so,
on the day that I learned that Anais was dead, I unfolded the two
pages of that old letter and found in the words a perfect portrait of
Anais Nin.

Why one writes, is a question I can answer easily, having asked it
so often of myself. I believe one writes because one has to create a
world in which one can live. I could not live in any of the worlds
offered to me, my parents', or American life in general, or the wars,
or any of my lovers' worlds. I had to create a world of my own, like
a climate, a country, an atmosphere in which I could breathe,
reign, and recreate my self destroyed by living. That I believe is the
reason for every work of art. The artist is the only one who knows
the world is subjective, that there is a choice to be made, a selection
of the elements one will live with, love. It is a materialization, an
incarnation of our inner world. Then we hope to attract others into
it, to impose this particular vision and share it with others. When
the second stage is not reached, the brave artists continue nonethe-
less. The others—you and me—occasionally lose heart. But the few
moments of communication with the world, with others, is worth
the pain, for when it is achieved it is in terms of your true self.

Now there are easier ways of communicating, directly through
human relationships, but it is not the same: it is not in terms of our
inner reality, on our own terms, by way of our own language. We
also write to make our life heightened, bearable, and more infinite.
We write to lure and enchant our lovers. We write to serenade
them. We write to taste life twice, in the moment, and in retro-
spection. We write, like Proust, to render all of it eternal and to
persuade ourselves that we are eternal. We write to be able to tran-
scend our life, to reach the space beyond it. We write to be able to
speak, to be able to explore all our secret and hidden selves,

*or we write like Genet, to rebel against the world, and to destroy
it, or we write like {Henry} Miller to throw bombs at it, or we
write to make a larger world, as I often do, when I feel strangled by
the pettiness, or the constrictions, restrictions, taboos, lies, falsities . . .*

    *Shall I go on . . . or have I said enough to encourage you? But I
only want to encourage you if it means that much to you, if you
breathe through writing, cry out through writing. Otherwise, don't
write. It is ill paid, it is non-commercial, and it is completely off
beat with the trend of the times, which is supplanting the image
and as far as writing goes, going the way of Barbarian epochs . . .
back to non-speech, primitive images, etc. Well, America is primitive. It hasn't much use for language. But if you write for the reasons I suggest, then you have to. When I don't, I feel my world
shrinking. I feel I am in a prison. I feel I lose my fire, my life, and
my color. It should be a necessity, as the sea needs to move. I call it
breathing.*

Years later, I got a postcard from Anais that had been forwarded
all over Europe when I was living there. "So sorry you didn't let me
know where to reach you," she wrote. "I published my letter to you
about why we write in Volume Five of the *Diaries,* but I couldn't
mention that it was written to you without your permission." I
smiled with amusement when I looked up the letter and compared it
with the original. Of course Anais had improved upon reality—a
word here, a phrase there . . . just enough to make the language sing.

Now the breathing has stopped. But the words of Anais Nin sus-
tain her fire, her life, and her color.

I recall the last time I saw her. I was visiting New York for the
first time, and she invited me to her apartment in Greenwich Village. She looked pale yet fiercely strong, poetically earnest almost to
the point of self-mockery, charming and generous and full of gossip.
We talked about Gore Vidal, Henry Miller, Maya Deren, and Kenneth Anger. We also talked about Susan Sontag, whom I had
known in high school and who was then emerging as a well-known
public figure.

Anais and I took a stroll in Washington Square, and I remember
how she beamed with pleasure when people turned to look at her.
The *Diaries* were a great success. Gone were the days when she had

Portrait of Anais Nin, *by Claude Michel Seren, 1977*

printed her own books on a hand press or entrusted them to Dutton, who wouldn't keep them in print, or to a small Denver publisher, who couldn't keep them in the bookstores. For all the years I had known Anais she had wanted to be famous. She knew the most controversial figures of her era. She had been everywhere and she had done everything. She even became something of a "personality," but literary celebrity had evaded her. She was known, but she was not renowned, and I suspect that even more than wanting to be published and admired, Anais wanted to be be exalted. Eventually, a rare constellation of events changed her life. During the rise of the women's movement she became a particularly attractive figure. And so, at last, she rose to international recognition.

Fame suited her. She had perfected the grand manner, and she possessed exactly the right blend of accessibility and aloofness that marks all true public figures. It was glorious to be with her during her moment of triumph.

Then almost at once, as if her long siege upon an indifferent public had fatally exhausted her, a new battle began with cancer. She fought hard but she lost.

James Leo Herlihy went on to write *Blue Denim, All Fall Down, Midnight Cowboy,* and *Season of the Witch.* Then, as if disappointed with the infinite problems and complexities of success, he slouched back to Los Angeles and fell silent. As for me, I filled the bottom drawer of my desk with a stack of unpublished manuscripts and set off for San Francisco, where I formed a theater company. Then one day a letter came from Jamie. With it was a print of an elegant painting of Anais Nin. Jamie had written on the back: "I thought you might like this picture of our mutual friend." Today it hangs next to an unforgettable photograph that Jill Krementz gave me of Anais in all her majesty, wearing a cape and looking wonderfully theatrical as she reclines on the grass in Washington Square.

"But the *few moments* of communication with the world, with others, is worth the pain," she had written to me long ago. Her few moments are over. Now the pain of her loss goes on. But as James Leo Herlihy told me: "It will be okay, my friend. We miss her, but don't forget: she had it all."

SCHOOL DAYS:
SUSAN SONTAG

In November of 1977 I read an interview with Susan Sontag in *The Soho Weekly News,* where I was the classical music editor. Her bitter memories of her adolescence saddened me as I realized how much she seemed to have changed since I had known her in high school.

I don't recall how or when I met Susan. She was ahead of me in school and we didn't take any classes together, but we were friends during the year before she graduated and went off to Berkeley. Even then, when most young people were either childishly cute or thoroughly undistinguished in appearance, Susan was marvelously handsome: intensely dark and solemn, her eyes filled with excep-

Susan Sontag, as pictured in a high school yearbook

tional intelligence, her thick black hair shorter and curlier than it is today, and her delicately shaped lips always poised to let loose a spectacular flood of articulate ideas that both fascinated and infuriated me.

Our friendship was strangely impersonal. But in Southern California that wasn't unusual. We didn't talk about our families. I recall meeting her severely sophisticated mother only once. And Susan never came to my home because I was forbidden visitors. She lived in a large house in Toluca Lake, a wealthy neighborhood in the Valley, but we never met there. I didn't know her father's profession, and I didn't know that she had been born in New York City and spent her childhood in Arizona. In fact, I didn't know anything about her personal history, nationality, or religion, and she knew nothing of mine. In New York, many people have a profound interest in their European heritage, but in California there has always been an atmosphere of historical anonymity, as if everyone had been recently hatched out of the Pacific Ocean. Perhaps this insistence upon personal secrecy comes out of the mythology of the motion picture industry. In those days it was commonplace for people to have a couple of professional names—even people without any apparent profession. Students at school who acted in films were known to us by one name and to the public by another. In those days, actors like Meryl Streep and Ellen Burstyn would have adopted stage names, like "Judy Garland" and "Doris Day." In Southern California then, the transformation of personality was taken for granted, and we simply did not discuss the complexities of our personal histories. There were too many divorces, too many altered biographies, too many people who had come west to escape the past.

But Susan and I did discuss ideas. I always fought on behalf of intuition and feeling, while Susan believed in the supremacy of reason. Those debates were often intense, long and heated. Her articulateness, keen intelligence, and remarkably broad reading experience inevitably plunged me into my habitual feeling of self-consciousness. But she challenged me and forced me to defend my ideas, insisting that I read an endless list of novels and essays that I eventually became capable of using to fortify my own viewpoint. And I introduced her to a few writers, like Federico García Lorca and Djuna

Barnes. Eventually I learned enough to win a few of our intellectual battles, which was not easy with such a formidable opponent as Susan.

I owe Susan a great deal, and I suspect that our curious and brief friendship in high school was also significant for her. We were both outsiders, much removed from the coyness and pettiness of our generation. We didn't have anyone else with whom to share our developing ideas. And so we became friends more by default than by choice.

When I read the 1977 interview with Susan in the *Soho News,* in which she spoke disparagingly of her high school days, I was a bit sad. She was correct, of course, in recalling the superficiality of our education, the "reader's digest" approach to everything, but she failed to recall some people who, I believe, were important in her life. I remember a teacher of social studies who befriended Susan and frequently discussed politics with her. This teacher intimidated me: he was rather cerebral and fierce and aggressively liberal in a day when it took immense courage to be politically radical. I gained some degree of political consciousness through those discussions, but to a very great extent I was put off by his approach to society, which lacked compassion and a high regard for culture. Susan, however, seemed to thrive on these discussions.

Another faculty member—I'll call her Ms. T— provided Susan and me with the opportunity of exercising our eccentricities by putting together a literary magazine. At the time, Susan was the editor of the high school newspaper, so she was in charge: she picked the poems and stories and wrote an introduction to the magazine. I remember the long hours she and I spent in Ms. T's classroom, typing the stencils and mimeographing the pages. Finally, we spread the pages on the desks and then collated them. By late afternoon, we were ready to staple the pages between covers. That day was particularly memorable for me because my first story appeared in that mimeographed magazine. It was called "There's Always Another Hill."

Ms. T was a literary mentor, but she was also memorable because of something else. She was an attractive young woman who often dated a good-looking athletic young man who also taught at the school. I don't recall that Susan and I ever speculated about sexual matters, but if we did so we surely assumed, as everyone else did, that Ms. T and her masculine boyfriend were the quintessential heterosexual couple. I don't remember exactly how the subject came up, I just know that one day Ms. T mentioned rather casually that she was homosexual, as if she wanted us to know about it. Perhaps she recognized that we were outsiders who would not be dismayed and would not breach her confidence. Perhaps she knew something then that we did not know. Whatever her reason, she explained that she and the gym teacher dealt with the bigotry of the world by pretending to be lovers. For two high school students who lived in the midst of the film industry, that explanation was not very shocking. But I was exhilarated to realize that these two teachers thought enough of our maturity to tell us about their controversial sexual attitudes, in much the same way that our social studies teacher had discussed his radical political ideas.

During her senior year in high school, Susan was an usher at the renowned Concerts on the Roof series at the Wilshire-Ebell Theater in Los Angeles, in order to attend what was at that time the best series of modern musical events in the West. Susan arranged for me to show up just before the performance and let me slip into the empty seat next to her. The last concert we saw together was memorable and influential for me, like our brief but remarkable friendship. Alice Mock performed *Pierrot Lunaire* by Arnold Schönberg. The conductor was a very young man named Robert Craft.

Soon Susan graduated and, like many in the brief and intense friendships of youth, we abruptly lost touch. I went on to create school shows and to present film programs, and I even won a measure of popularity. I made two or three new friends, but they could not replace Susan. They drew energy and ideas from me without giving very much in return.

I did not hear anything about Susan Sontag for many years. And then one day I opened *Time* magazine and saw a familiar face. I was delighted by her success and immediately wrote a note congratulating her.

Many years later, when I was at a performance of *Otello* at the Metropolitan Opera, I spotted Susan sitting on the aisle a few rows in front of me. Though we had not seen each other since our adolescence, I approached her and said: "Hello, Susan . . . do you remember who I am?"

For a moment she seemed annoyed by the intrusion, but then a fragile and rare expression of friendliness crept into her stern face. There was even a trace of shyness as she gazed up at me, shaking her head as if confused by the remote familiarity of my face.

A NIGHT AT THE CINEMA: DALTON TRUMBO

"People seem to forget that World War I is fifty years old and how very much we've changed since those days," Dalton Trumbo rasps, pumping on his cigarette holder and reclining easily in an over-stuffed chair. He smiles professionally and speaks in a rusty voice that has the firm press and fine resonance of an orator's despite its whiskeyed timbre.

Trumbo is the epitome of the beautiful old man. Dour, bohemian, sagacious. He speaks entirely without effort or hesitation, giving his conversation the tone of a prepared statement. But his sincerity is attested to not just by the candor in his beautiful eyes,

Dalton Trumbo

but also by his tumultuous history. He has championed a number of unfashionable causes during his long life, and he has paid a high price for his opinions.

In 1947, Trumbo was one of ten Hollywood writers and directors (the Hollywood Ten) who were summoned to Washington to testify before the House Un-American Activities Committee. With his colleagues, Trumbo refused to disclose to the committee whether he was or had ever been a member of the Communist party. When I recall that moment, Trumbo stares off into the past. "I refused to spill my private truth," he mutters, as if the pain of that incident were still tormenting him. "Being a public figure doesn't make you public property."

Now he falls silent. Even in the liberal atmosphere of the mid-1960s, when this conversation with Dalton Trumbo took place, the aftershocks of those horrendous years of purges, the incredible abuse of talented people, overtake us. The panic of the accused. The betrayal by colleagues or, even worse, the utter silence of friends. A naive public outraged by mere gossip. A time of fearsome patriotism. The hearings. And then the destroyed careers. In one moment, the whole catastrophe of the witch-hunts descends upon us. I try to imagine what this remarkable old man is thinking and feeling. But as I gaze at him, I am suddenly taken back to the San Fernando Valley and the home of John Howard Lawson, another of the Hollywood Ten.

I strain to recapture the image of Lawson, sitting in his library, a pipe burning in an ashtray, solemn and only slightly tolerant of the intrusion when his preadolescent daughter, Mandy, brings me into the room and introduces me. His seriousness both impresses and embarrasses me. He makes some remark, hardly looking at me, and then waves us away as he returns to his work. I hesitate and peer intently into his sacrosanctity, profoundly touched to be so close to a real writer, awed by the many books that surround him, and a bit sorry not to have such a father of my own.

I remember the Lawson house on a hill, with people and dogs hurrying in and out the doors—a friendly and rather unruly place except for the sanctuary of Lawson's library. But I don't recall how I met Mandy, though it was probably at school. She was very much

John Howard Lawson

involved in youth politics and asked me to join an organization called American Youth for Democracy. We sat on the lawn in the schoolyard with our brown lunchbags, and I listened to the dissident speeches. But I could not find my way into the heart of these ideas. I, too, was dissatisfied with the world. I was a loner and a misfit, so I naturally had a strong concern for the underdog. I was terrified by the little I understood about the political life of the times. I had recently read the transcripts of hearings held in Sacramento aimed at the removal of teachers with unpopular political associations, and I was utterly outraged. I was concerned as only the very young can be concerned with issues such as hunger and racism and fanaticism. But what I heard that afternoon at the meeting of American Youth for Democracy did not touch me. To the contrary, I felt that I was simply hearing a different kind of fanaticism. I didn't care what people named their political ideas, and I didn't care who had the power that seemed to be the constant source of conflict. What I did care about was the unrelenting existence of deprivation and pain in the world.

Dalton Trumbo shifts in his chair, and his sigh of discomfort brings me back to the hotel room. The activist screenwriter is now an old man, and I am a journalist for *The Chicago Tribune*. In 1976, not too many years after our conversation, Trumbo died. But happily, by that time his reputation as an artist had been reestablished. The seventies were his good years, a time when America embraced many of the dissidents that it had once abhorred and abused. Trumbo no longer had to write under an assumed name in order to make a living. In fact, an excellent film version of his book *Johnny Got His Gun* was released in 1971 to very favorable reviews. Now, once again, he could speak his mind.

"Sure," he reminisces bitterly, "we could have taken the Fifth Amendment, but we didn't want it that way. We were far more idealistic and even more stubborn than you kids are today. For us, either it was the First, or our Constitution was impotent."

In 1947, civil disobedience was almost unheard of. The mere accusation of political nonconformity was sufficient to destroy people both personally and professionally. The aura of suspicion and unreasonable nationalism was so intense in the days of Joe McCarthy that Trumbo was looked upon as a traitor. It was simply inconceivable to the people in the film industry that anyone with Trumbo's "good name and track record" would expose himself to adverse publicity and scandal over a mere political ideal. News stories of the period, overblown with journalistic indignation, easily convinced the public that Trumbo, Lawson, and the others of the Hollywood Ten had smuggled "tainted viewpoints" and "shameful philosophies" into the dialogue of the film scripts they had written for Hollywood's unsuspecting moguls. One of the most damning bits of "evidence" against them, for instance, was a piece of dialogue in which a starving young character melodramatically intones: "God in heaven, the day must come when there is enough food in this world for everyone!"

Dalton Trumbo and his colleagues were convicted of contempt of Congress for refusing to answer the committee's questions. Soon after their conviction, the leading Hollywood producers, in a burst of patriotism, blacklisted "the unfriendly ten" and all others who might refuse to talk to Congress—a list that eventually grew to about two hundred and fifty names. Trumbo's prosperous career as a major film writer ended abruptly, and he and the others became nameless talents, selling their scripts on the black market pseudonymously—a situation so tragically ridiculous that Woody Allen eventually made a film about it called *The Front.*

In 1950 Dalton Trumbo went to jail, serving ten months in the Federal Correctional Institution in Ashland, Kentucky, for refusing to testify before the committee.

"What about young people during all of this? Didn't any college people or artists come to your defense?" I ask.

Trumbo gives me the curious, long gaze of an elder who is stupefied by the naïveté of the young. He refills my glass and slowly lights another cigarette, and then he explains: "We were film writers. Do you understand that the movies have only become respectable in the past few years? In those days we were considered mere hacks who were getting too much money for knocking out mediocre westerns in the L.A. sunshine. Nobody ever listened to the dialogue coming at them from the screen. No one ever bothered to analyze the structure of a movie. The *intellectuals,*" he hisses with disdain, "... they were in the universities, talking theory and promising the

Great American Novel that never came. They were in the sacrosanct literary quarterlies, unsoiled by the notion of being *working* writers.

"They always looked down their noses at us. So when we were arrested and became the center of political controversy, rather than coming to our aid as they would today—testifying, marching, and so forth—they said to themselves: 'Why them? Why not us? After all, we're the intellectuals!' And I don't think that they ever really forgave us for stealing their thunder. Envy is a terrible thing."

In and out of prison, in Hollywood and during two years of self-imposed exile in Mexico, Dalton Trumbo wrote thirty movies under various pseudonyms. In 1957, during the Academy Awards ceremonies, "Robert Rich" was announced as the author of the year's best original screenplay, *The Brave Ones*. No one came forward to accept the award. Writer Robert Rich was, in fact, Dalton Trumbo—who had managed to smuggle another unconventionally candid motion picture about racism and inequity before the slumberous American moviegoer.

Trumbo outlived McCarthy, who died of cancer in 1957. The blacklist died with him. In 1960, director Otto Preminger openly signed Trumbo to write the screenplay for *Exodus*. It was his first publicly acknowledged writing assignment in a decade. Among Dalton Trumbo's various screenplays are *Kitty Foyle, A Guy Named Joe, Thirty Seconds over Tokyo* (often cited for its subversive undertones), *Our Vines Have Tender Grapes* (another perilously political film), *Spartacus* (which arduously avoids the social issues fundamental to its historical context), *Lonely Are the Brave,* and *The Fixer.*

Perhaps the most widely regarded of Trumbo's efforts is the World War I novel (and subsequent film) *Johnny Got His Gun,* a highly self-conscious and strongly antiwar novel published in 1939, at the outset of another global conflict.

"I can remember as a seventh grader watching the seniors going off to war," Trumbo recalls. "It was easily the most enthusiastic thing I've ever seen. Flags! Marching bands! Real joy! After all, my God, the kids were going to Paris! Fifty years ago that kind of thing was a miracle in America. That war made a very, very strong impression on me. But then in 1933, fifteen years later, I ran across a newspaper story from the London *Times*. It was about a British major who had been wounded in 1918 and who had been reported to his family as missing in action, though, in fact, he had been hospitalized. After years of treatment, the major died and the British army admitted that it had withheld information about the identity of the soldier because his condition had been so *absolutely terrible* . . . yes, so absolutely terrible, they said, that it would have been quite impossible for the family to see him. Well that story arouses one's imagination, now doesn't it! I mean, after all, what condition was this man in that they didn't even dare tell his own family that he was still alive?"

For a moment Trumbo puffs thoughtfully on his cigarette. "About a year later, in 1934, the Prince of Wales—later the Duke of Windsor—was visiting a Canadian military hospital. At the end of a corridor there was a door marked No Admittance. When the prince asked to be admitted, the officials said that they wished he would not make that request. He insisted, and of course they opened the door and let him pass. When he came out, according to the press, he was weeping. Yes . . . weeping. He was asked why he was upset, and he then told the reporters that he had seen in this little closed-off room at the end of a corridor a man who was so frightfully mutilated by war that the only way he could possibly communicate with him was to kiss him on the forehead."

Trumbo presses his eyes closed as if to push away a terrible vision. Then he looks off into the air and smiles very faintly, making a curious little sound which is perhaps an expression of dismay, almost the trace of a bitter laugh.

"So," he continues dramatically, "these two very tragic stories worked in my mind for about five years. Like recurrent nightmares, they came and went, prodding me as if they somehow meant something beyond themselves, as if they were Apocryphal in some strange way I could not yet comprehend . . . a decree about things to come." He pauses for just a moment, and then he says in a matter of fact tone: "Those feelings resulted in the book *Johnny Got His Gun*."

There is a long pause. Then, almost incongruously, Dalton Trumbo says: "I was born in Colorado in 1905. I started as a reader in the story department at Warner Brothers in 1936. I had no intention of becoming a subject of controversy. I just wanted to make movies. But in the 1930s we were in the midst of a terrible economic situation. It was an era when the political affiliations of people sometimes contradicted their actions. For instance, when a company foreclosed on a farm, the sale was usually held right there on the property, and suddenly peaceful, normally conservative farmers from miles around would show up with their shotguns. These Midwestern conservatives would buy the team of mules for two dollars and give the animals back to the bankrupt farmer. They bought the land for perhaps forty-five dollars and gave it back to its owner. Those foreclosures and the way farmers reacted to them represented a small revolution of sorts—people defying an illogical law. And it was conducted, this action of civil disobedience, by people who were usually very conservative in their politics and morals. So there had been a definite change in the credibility of law and order and the righteousness of our American political system. We had seen from the Depression that our methods were not as perfect as we had been led to believe. We were fallible . . . and that frightened us. American romanticism was vanishing as I grew up and people moved to the cities and communications became faster and far less idealized. By the 1930s I had already worked for eight hard years on the night shift of a bakery in Los Angeles. And that face-to-face realization of my own impotence as part of the work force changed me as it did so many other kids of my generation, who had come from their gentle rural worlds to the sweatshops of the American cities."

Now Trumbo pauses and laughs. "I suppose you have heard some rumors that I have been associated with many radical causes in my life. Well, you know, that's because I'm such an ardent believer in democracy. It all stems from the Democratic party, to tell you the truth. It was in 1924 that it started. I was nineteen when the national convention of the Democratic party was held. And do you know . . . do you know what they wrote into their official political platform? Well, let me read it to you." He rummages momentarily into the pockets of his jumpsuit and comes up with a worn bit of paper. Adjusting his glasses he reads: "In the event of war, in which the manpower of the nation is drafted, all other resources should likewise be drafted. This will tend to discourage war by depriving it of its profits."

As he tucks the paper away, Dalton Trumbo looks at me shrewdly. "Well, you can just imagine the effect of a piece of propaganda like that on a boy of nineteen! I was totally swept away! It's quite close to socialism, you know. And," he grins with an irrepressible expression of youthful valor, "once that poison had been injected by the Democratic party, it ran through my veins for years and years. I'm not cured of it yet! I'm trying hard," he laughs, "but the flesh is weak!"

ADVENTURES IN FILM: FROM JEAN COCTEAU TO RON RICE

My years in San Francisco left me with memories of immense isolation, frantic effort, unheralded achievement, calamity, infuriating cultural indifference, and the debris of many delicate young lives—like the dancer who slashed his wrists and danced himself to death in his blood-splattered living room and like the friend who awakened in the middle of the night, kissed her husband, who strongly disapproved of her career in dance, went into the bathroom, where she took an overdose of barbiturates, and then returned to her husband's side to die while he slept.

I'm certain there was much ordinary happiness in San Francisco,

Jean Cocteau

but all I remember are the extremes: the desperation and the constant stream of remarkable people who passed through my life and kept me alive.

I have a vivid fantasy: Jean Cocteau sitting in his uniquely poised manner, classically reposed and thoughtful, his hair pushed back off his forehead as if artfully uncombed, and his quietly expressive and delicate long fingers drawn together in his lap. That impression remains a fantasy, but I also possess something quite real: a small collection of scribbled notes that flowed to me from time to time from Cocteau. "I demand a dark silence from my audience, a silence almost as violent as laughter," he once wrote in the margin of a drawing of Orpheus he made for me.

Cocteau's films established themselves in the dark world of which their creator speaks: a world I would visit repeatedly without the least sense of redundancy—experiencing and reexperiencing an idiom of cinema that, like poetry, possessed an unlimited number of levels and details to absorb me, to renew my excitement, and to enhance my perspective on the world.

I discovered Cocteau by accident. As a kid I became a foreign-film enthusiast, thanks to my foster father's admiration for Emil Jannings. One night he took me to a rare screening of the German film *The Last Laugh* at a tiny repertory cinema in Los Angeles called The Coronet. Though so-called art films were at that time little known by the public, I was instantly attracted to their imagination and daring. I began to go to The Coronet regularly. One night the program included a film called *Carmen,* with Vivian Romance and Jean Marais. I thought I was going to hear an opera; instead, I saw a drama based on the story of the infamous gypsy. *Carmen* was entertaining, but the film on the program that utterly fascinated me was Jean Cocteau's *Beauty and the Beast.*

Suddenly Cocteau became my hero. I read his writings and searched out all his films. And eventually I got up the courage to write to him. Astonishingly, he responded with a note and a drawing.

From that time, Cocteau and I exchanged letters. I only regret that I never met him. By the time I managed to get to France, he

Drawing by Jean Cocteau

was already dead. I had a dreadful feeling of loss when I visited Chapelle Saint Blaise des Simples at Milly-la-Forêt—a tiny fisherman's chapel in Provence that he had decorated with frescoes. The delightful images conjured up his presence, and I abruptly realized he was truly gone and that I would never come face to face with this person who had greatly influenced me.

My obsession with Jean Cocteau had an elaborate history. More than a decade before my trip to France, I had established The Contemporary Center in San Francisco, where I organized a Jean Cocteau film festival. In celebration of the occasion, Cocteau sent an "open letter to the friends of my films":

> *You well know that the children of our spirit leave us and run around the world forgetting that they were born of us. Here is some good news: I have learned that four of my forgetful children want to live in San Francisco and meet friends who are younger than their father. Greet my dear children for me (if they still remember me) and wish them luck. From the bottom of my heart, I thank all of you for giving them your hospitality.*

As poet, novelist, essayist, cinematographer, playwright, choreog-

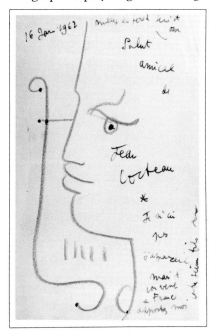

Drawing by Jean Cocteau

rapher, painter, and spokesperson for the illustrious group of composers known as Les Six, Cocteau lit up the whole horizon of twentieth-century art in France. When I was a young man, he seemed to me utterly remarkable for his versatility and eloquence. "Dear Friend," he wrote to me one Christmas, "works of art transcend us and through them we make our voyage out, we assume an eternal form, one of strength and youth." I believed completely in that doctrine. I was encouraged by his example to venture into a world of imagination that both beckoned and intimidated me.

In Cocteau's eclectic mentality I found a model of the artist that greatly attracted me, and I found a new world through his novel *Les Enfants terribles* and such films as *Beauty and the Beast* and *Blood of a Poet*. Through his influence I came to expect something exceptional from the motion picture. He prepared me for my experience of the art film, of the kind of cinema that Dalton Trumbo and John Howard Lawson wanted to create: films that possess more vitality and significance than the often perishable Hollywood movies on which I had grown up.

The film series at The Contemporary Center was only partly a result of Cocteau's influence. I also went in search of his American counterparts. Bruce Connor was among the original organizers of the series, and we often showed his *Movie* to bewildered audiences that could not understand how someone could legitimately create a film that was a collage—entirely composed of preexisting footage from commercials and cartoons. Another filmmaker who worked with us was Bruce Baillie, whose earliest films were premiered at The Contemporary Center. There was also a visit by Maya Deren, who stood in a spotlight in front of the screen—her great halo of auburn hair glowing as if it were on fire—as she talked about her extraordinary films.

Perhaps the most memorable premiere at the theater was for a remarkably strange feature film by Ron Rice, then a completely unknown cinematographer who had walked into the office one day and said, "I want to show you something." What he showed us was a film that was so totally new for its time that we really didn't know what to make of it. The picture was called *The Flower Thief,* and it starred a newcomer by the name of Taylor Mead. It was September

Ron Rice

Taylor Mead

1960, and members of the Beat Generation were still hanging out in San Francisco's North Beach district, in places like the City Lights bookstore, Vesuvio's, and Miss Smith's Tea Room. *The Flower Thief* emerged from the final days of that quickly fading cultural scene. In the words of Ron Rice, "the film shows some highs and lows in the life of a poet [Mead] living in North Beach. This film is a true cinematic expression of the 'hip' and 'beat' philosophy. I have shown some of the North Beach inhabitants in natural and surrealistic surroundings without a moral to intrude upon the action. Primary attention has been given to spontaneous antics, without too much contrived staging—all too common in the planned film."

The Flower Thief soon became a cult classic. Its lack of polish and its technical flaws and improvisational mood made it a welcome alternative to slick Hollywood films. Critic Sheldon Renan has called Ron Rice "one of the major talents of the New American Cinema." He was also a strangely abrupt and friendly man whose utter lack of grace was somehow endearing. His intensity and drive were extraordinary. He constantly battled to find funds for his projects. And he lived on the edge of extinction.

After the premiere of *The Flower Thief*, I didn't see Ron Rice again. In 1964, he went to Mexico to start a new project. In December he became ill and was admitted to a hospital in Acapulco, where he died of bronchial pneumonia.

The Flower Thief began a brilliant underground career for actor Taylor Mead. His second role was in an experimental feature, *Lemon Hearts,* by Vernon Zimmerman, the man who had introduced us to Ron Rice. *Lemon Hearts* also premiered at our theater, in 1962. Mead played the same sort of bent waif that he had played in *The Flower Thief.* He was becoming something of a celebrity in San Francisco, until he went east and joined Andy Warhol's Factory, becoming one of the first stars of the underground cinema. Years later I would run into him late at night in New York City, a portable radio pressed to his ear. He sometimes looked out at me through an immense pharmaceutical haze. "You're the one who showed it, aren't you?" he would whisper with a curiously sad smile momentarily lighting his perpetually tragic face. Then he would press the little radio to his ear and slowly fade away.

ADVENTURES IN THE PERFORMING ARTS: FROM ANNA HALPRIN TO ERICK HAWKINS

The first time I saw Anna Halprin perform, in 1960, I knew she was a rare and important artist. The dance was called *The Prophetess,* and it was a strongly emotional duet for Halprin and her nine- or ten-year-old daughter, Daria. Though her choreographic style was influenced by Doris Humphrey, Charles Weidman, and Martha Graham, *The Prophetess* was emphatically original, and Halprin's dancing was flawless. I came away from that performance in San Francisco knowing that I had just seen one of the most important choreographers of the era.

Anna Halprin came out of the dramatic tradition of modern

Anna Halprin

dance, having trained in New York at a time when the Graham-Humphrey-Weidman idioms were much in fashion. After her marriage to landscape architect Lawrence Halprin, Anna moved to the relative artistic isolation of San Francisco, where she joined a former Graham dancer, Welland Lathrop, and founded a dance school and performing company.

By the time I moved to San Francisco from Los Angeles, in 1954, the Halprin-Lathrop Studio had become a major center of dance, and I sometimes sat in on classes and rehearsal at their Union Street studio. My attraction to dancing was strong, but my experience as a dancer was very limited. I had taken some classes and I had even tried my hand at choreography, staging shows and cabarets. I had also done some improvisational solos at various amateur theaters in Los Angeles. But I had had none of the arduous training that dance requires. I don't recall exactly how my fascination with dancing began. But I suspect that as a child I discovered dancing not in films or on the stage but within my own body, for movement has always been an intrinsic power in my life. Though the origin of my lifelong interest in dancing is only dimly remembered, I know for certain that the first choreographers I met and admired were Ruth St. Denis and Lester Horton. Their imprint on my childhood sensibility and my later choreographic activity was immense. Despite my decision to be a writer, I was persistently drawn to Miss Ruth's studio on Ventura Boulevard and to the storefront theater run by Lester Horton on Melrose Avenue in Los Angeles. I could not escape the attraction of dancing.

So when I arrived in San Francisco, I got it into my head that I wanted to try to make a living by teaching dance. I managed to find a job at one of those neighborhood schools that give classes in baton twirling, tap dancing, and ballet. I felt like a fool when I climbed to the third floor and applied for a job, but I knew more about modern dance than anybody else at the school, so they hired me. I summoned all my courage and stepped in front of a classroom full of people, and I began to invent a dance idiom straight out of my head. Everyone at the studio wanted to dance like Gene Kelly or Ginger Rogers, but I wanted to teach them to dance like Anna Halprin.

For daring people, those were difficult years in San Francisco. Even the most talented of the Beat writers were largely ignored and had to migrate to New York before they could attain substantial recognition. It was something of a marvel that Halprin was able to do the work she did—that she could create innovative theater of real significance in a city that claimed a cultural concern it did not truly possess. The renowned Actors Workshop and several other organizations that aspired to be innovative had a terrible time attracting sponsors and audiences. And Anna Halprin, as far as I know, was among the first experimental artists in San Francisco.

Dances like *The Prophetess* were highly accessible by today's standards, but in the late 1950s there was almost no audience for modern dance in San Francisco. At that time the only dance events that attracted an audience were the San Francisco Ballet's annual Christmas presentation of *The Nutcracker* and visits by New York–based ballet companies. People who were put off by even the most narrative of Halprin's works were totally unprepared for a radical new direction that her work began to take in the early 1960s. Her transformation from narrative choreographer to avant-garde experimenter came after she had left Lathrop's studio and had gone into virtual retirement at her home in Kentfield, where her famous architect husband had built an outdoor dance deck that provided the only basis for her continued work with a small coterie of talented students. Her close association with Merce Cunningham, who had given a series of annual classes at the Halprin-Lathrop Studio for several years, obviously had a strong impact on Halprin. The dances that resulted from this influence, and from her own experimentation, were based on nonrepresentational movements welded by her theatrical intuition into entirely abstract dances operating with the most insistent, satisfying, and curious logic. But only a few invited guests ever saw these experiments. Now and again Anna's ardor for dance would resurface and she would experiment with the natural environment that surrounded her dance deck, asking a few friends to come out to Marin County and see her efforts. But she no longer gave public performances.

By this time several refugees from the tap dance school, where I had begun my career as a teacher, had joined with me in founding a dance company at a marvelous redwood and glass church, built in 1906, that we converted into a theater called The Contemporary

Center. That publicly neglected, constantly embattled, and poverty-stricken theater became the proving ground for some outstanding talents and the arena for many major cultural events.

I was often among the guests invited to Kentfield to see Anna's new dances, and I became very enthusiastic about what she was doing. At my urging she decided to present some of her new pieces at The Contemporary Center. The theater was made available to her for sufficient time for her completely to choreograph *The Flower-burger, Birds of America, Mr. and Mrs. Mouse,* and *The Three-Legged Stool* on the stage where all of these landmark dances were soon to be premiered. The music critic of *The San Francisco Examiner* noted that Halprin had "surely given the weirdest dance concert this city has ever seen." It was also one of the most important. In the space of less than a month of creative effort—with dancers Daria Halprin, John Graham, and A. A. Leath—Anna Halprin had produced an evening of dance that was to become a milestone in twentieth-century dance.

With the incentive of this success, Halprin relaunched her dance career and began a series of classes and dance concerts that involved several performers who would eventually make important inroads elsewhere, including James Waring, Simone Forti, Yvonne Rainer, Meredith Monk, and Trisha Brown. Halprin's own choreography did not gain wide recognition until the premiere of *Parades and Changes* at Hunter College in New York City on April 21, 1967. Unfortunately, most of the hoopla surrounded the nudity, which Halprin championed and which had won her company a scandalous reputation when it toured Europe and appeared naked on Swedish television. The real importance of *Parades and Changes,* however, was that it worked in an idiom we now call "performance art."

Anna Halprin's history ranges across the entire spectrum of modern dance, from the first generation of Graham, Humphrey, and Weidman to the current generation of postmodern choreographers. Out of the upheaval of her personal life in Kentfield, Halprin built an isolated dance community during the social upheavals of the 1960s and 1970s. This community became a center for those attracted to the arts rather than to the artless mystique of the Haight-Ashbury scene. Highly creative choreographers came and went through Halprin's dance community. Meanwhile, Halprin herself

THE CONTEMPORARY DANCERS FOUNDATION presents
November 29, 30, December 1, 8:30 P M

THE ANN HALPRIN DANCERS WORKSHOP

DIRECTOR — ANN HALPRIN
ASSOCIATE — A. A. LEATH

DANCERS — JOHN GRAHAM . ANN HALPRIN
DARIA HALPRIN . A.A. LEATH

ARTISTIC CONSULTANT, COSTUMES
SET —
JO LANDOR

LIGHTING DESIGN — PATRICK
HICKEY

MUSICIANS — TERRY RILEY, WARNER JEPSON
CREW — SHIRLEY BROWN, JULIE STEWART

STORY — POEMS USED IN "FLOWERBURGER" by RICHARD BRAUTIGAN
"MR & MRS. MOUSE" FROM JAMES BROUGHTON'S
"RITES OF WOMEN"

MUSIC — IN FIRST SERIES OF DANCES — JOHN CAGE — WINTER
MUSIC
LAMONTE YOUNG —
STRING TRIO.

DANCES * BIRDS OF AMERICA
1 *   or
GARDENS WITHOUT WALLS
intermission
2 * THE FLOWERBURGER
3 * MR. & MRS. MOUSE

DESIGN
LAWRENCE HALPRIN

Program announcement by The Contemporary Center

plummeted forward, evolving a communal choreographic method
dependent on highly personalized and improvised actions that departed entirely from what had previously been regarded as proper
dance movement. In many ways, probably, Anna Halprin is the most
radical personality in dance in the second half of the twentieth century—the Isadora Duncan of our time—for her evolutionary process
appears to be unending. Her students have gone on to create radical
but relatively stable dance attitudes and forms, while Halprin herself
continues a perilous nose dive into the unknown.

Many dance and theater events were presented at The Contemporary Center during its troubled decade of existence. Charles Weidman restaged *Lynch Town* and his James Thurber dances for us. One
day while he and I were having lunch at a local cafe, I proudly told

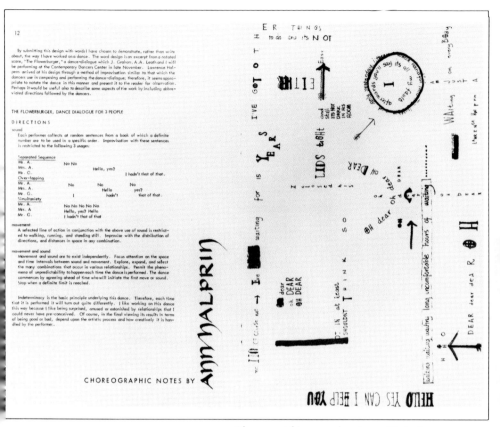

Choreographic notes by Anna Halprin

the waitress who he was and how fortunate we were to have him visiting the city. When she asked him where he was from, Weidman smiled that innocent smile of his and, instead of saying New York City, where he had long worked and lived, he simply said, "Nebraska."

The National Dancers of Ceylon spent a week at our theater, and we were always astonished when they knelt in meditation before each performance and then, transfigured by their prayers, went on stage, where they would suddenly open up like oriental fans.

There were also performances by Spanish dancers, Russian dancers, and many renowned modern dance companies. Jean Erdman brought her production called *The Coach With the Six Insides*—a landmark theater work based on *Finnegans Wake*.

One of the first American productions of Jean Genet's *The Maids* took place at The Contemporary Center, and Jack Gelber's hyperrealist play *The Connection* had its San Francisco premiere there. We lost our shirts presenting the original Los Angeles company in a delightful little musical called *The Fantasticks.* It was considered so bizarre that it played to empty houses for a week and was an utter flop.

My own choreographic efforts melded with a wide variety of guest performances. Now and again I moonlighted. I directed Jules Irving in his "dance" role as Lucky in the Actors Workshop production of *Waiting for Godot,* and I staged programs for the PBS affiliate in San Francisco, KQED. All of this greatly diversified and experimental activity depended upon the creative efforts and hard work of the dozens of exceptionally talented and devoted people who helped to create The Contemporary Center: dancers, teachers, photographers, musicians, technicians, painters, writers, poets, and composers, as well as countless people who did a great deal of work just to keep the doors of the theater open. Today some of these friends are gone. I remember Ansel Adams smiling broadly in the lobby, where he had mounted a small exhibition of photographs for the opening night of our season. There was also the memorable night when we premiered our production of *Man and His Desire.* Darius Milhaud was confined to a wheelchair, and he had to be laboriously carried up the fifteen steps of our theater so he could be present at this first staging of the famous score he had originally composed for Nijinsky. "But Diaghilev was never able to produce the ballet, because by that time Nijinsky was already quite mad. He insisted that mysterious enemies were trying to break his legs so he would not be able to dance," Milhaud confided one day when I was visiting him at his home at Mills College.

Many of the people I knew during those years in San Francisco have become international figures. I recall Tom Hutchings giving a world-premiere performance of Terry Riley's *Two Works for Piano* before an audience that couldn't have consisted of more than a dozen people. Terry, who had just returned from studying in Europe with Stockhausen, sat there bravely. A decade later we would meet again at a Columbia Records bash to celebrate the release of Terry's minimalist score *In C* and a soundscape I had produced with Shipen

Lebzelter and John McClure. Another unknown composer was there whose first album was also being commemorated. His name was Walter Carlos, and the record was called *Switched On Bach.* I remember feeling sorry for Carlos because everyone was saying that electronic Bach was silly and simply couldn't make it. Ah, yes.

One of my favorite memories of those San Francisco days is the image of Robin Wagner, meticulously dressed in a suit and tie—paint flying and staple gun stuttering away—as he put the final touches on the scenery he had designed for us. Having worked all day as a window decorator, he would rush into the theater and with almost no assistance turn pasteboard boxes and bits of wood—the only supplies we could afford—into brilliant stage images. He began as a designer at The Contemporary Center and created perhaps a dozen sets for us before his baroque and bizarre imagination was noticed by Herbert Blau of the San Francisco Actors Workshop. His first project for Blau was the production of *Waiting for Godot.* Then, after executing a succession of designs for the Actors Workshop, Robin went to New York, where he won great praise for his sets for *Hair, Jesus Christ, Superstar, Lenny, The Great White Hope,* and many other Broadway productions.

One day in 1960, two dancers from the San Francisco Ballet came to The Contemporary Center to talk about a new performing group they wanted to organize. They had had little or no prior experience as choreographers, but they were quite determined to create ballets that departed from the somewhat conservative stance of the local ballet company. One of them felt particularly passionate about doing dances that reflected his youthful ideals and adventurous ideas, ballets involving popular music and modern themes.

His name was Michael Smuin, and today he is a choreographer of international stature and the director of the San Francisco Ballet. The other young man was named Jeffrey Hobart, and he did most of the talking about business: explaining that Lew Christensen, the director of the San Francisco Ballet, had declined to sponsor their experimental enterprise. Smuin and Hobart hoped that The Contemporary Center would present the group's debut. I was hesitant to encourage them, because I had friends at the San Francisco Ballet

Robin Wagner (right) and Jamake Highwater

whom I didn't want to offend. I was especially fond of James Graham-Lujan, associate director of the ballet company, whose close association with the family of Federico García Lorca and whose translations of the Spanish poet's major plays had been the basis of our friendship. But Michael Smuin's intense belief in the new dance company ignited my own enthusiasm, and so I had to find some way of assisting the project.

Eventually a program of seven dances was presented by The Contemporary Center under the title Ballet 1960. Among the dancers were Sue Loyd, Roderick Drew, Terry Orr, Robert Gladstein, Fiona Fuerstner, Sailey Bailey, Zack Thompson, and Michael Smuin. Four Smuin ballets were premiered, the most expansive of which was the *Symphony in Jazz* and the most fascinating of which was a short trio called *Session* that was performed to the drumming of Ran Kaye.

Ballet 1960 was a hit; so eventually we presented Ballet 1961. The only dark moment associated with this otherwise luminous adventure in ballet was a call from Lew Christensen politely requesting that we avoid any mention of his ballet company in relation to these experimental programs. But the success of the venture must have changed some minds at the San Francisco Ballet. In the third year, quietly and without any mention that the venture had debuted at our theater, the San Francisco Ballet began to sponsor annual performances by the renegade dancers, under the direction of the innovative Michael Smuin.

In 1959 Erick Hawkins and Barbara Tucker gave three performances at The Contemporary Center of a full-evening dance work called *Here and Now with Watcher,* choreographed by Hawkins and performed to a score for timbre piano composed and played by Lucia Dlugoszewski.

Erick Hawkins has a special ability in his work to awaken the animal heritage in each of us. He reminds us that we are part of the animal kingdom. He sees the creature within us, and he is able to remember our infancy among the other animals. In his dances, that memory becomes clear to us. We recognize the essential human body within us, just as we recognize lions in the motion of lions, and birds in the motion of their flight.

Erick Hawkins

To find an animal body within himself, Hawkins tells me, he had to abandon narrative dancing—so much of it based on Greek myth and American themes—which he performed in his early days when he was the principal male dancer with the Martha Graham company. That kind of dancing was so dependent on the human psyche that it nearly ignored the human body. In those days, several major dancers—Cunningham, Erdman, and Hawkins—left Graham in order to get away from psychology and to reinvent dance according to a non-narrative, unsentimental approach that was already finding wide acceptance in the New York school of painting popularly represented by the works of Willem de Kooning, Robert Motherwell, and Jackson Pollock. Hawkins was part of the New York art scene of the 1940s, when Abstract Expressionism was being born, and he followed the impulse in his own manner, searching for a new principle of movement. Other dance revolutionaries of the same era, such as Merce Cunningham, were stupendously rational, having become convinced that classicism was the fundamental stuff from which everything in the arts evolves. But Hawkins was impelled by something else. As he puts it, "I wanted to find a physical and not a logical reason for dancing." He believed that he could find that reason in the mysterious body that exists without our bodies—in the spiritual body.

His involvement with the inner body led Hawkins to a premise about human movement from which everything most distinctive in his choreography flows. It is a premise so basic that it lies beyond and beneath matters of style and individuality in dancing. Hawkins has used that principle to create a succession of astoundingly clear dances.

"The spirit of Western man," Hawkins has said, "makes him think he has to work, to exert effort or force, and to conquer nature. Therefore dance teachers have passed on this erroneous notion about human movement—that you must *make* the movement happen, or dominate the movement through your will, or through 'hard work.'"

Hawkins makes no apologies for rejecting the entire mechanistic idea of dance technique, which he feels dominates ballet as well as much modern dance.

"The reason one is filled with wonder at the movement of most animals, like the cat family," he says, "is that they are always concentric and effortless. They have never been taught the fallacious *theory* of movement which, out of a partialness of the human mind, has inculcated ideas . . . that people should glory in being filled with effort and striving and a subtle Puritanism." In dance, as far as Erick Hawkins is concerned, "work is not the ultimate good."

I remember sitting in the dark auditorium of The Contemporary Center while Barbara Tucker and Erick Hawkins rehearsed *Here and Now with Watchers.* What I gradually came to understand in the darkness of that theater is that for Hawkins, dance is our only means of making visible our profoundest and simplest experiences of this ancient land we call America.

CONVERSATION WITH KARLHEINZ STOCKHAUSEN

It is a circular room perched atop a hill in Sausalito, California. From the sunshine-reflecting windows we can see San Francisco Bay, the dazzling white city, and a cluster of verdant islands scattered amidst the calm water. Sailboat wings catch the sunlight now and again, or a whitecap emerges from the placid bay. Karlheinz Stockhausen is standing by the window. The year is 1967. In his circular room is a circular table heaped with graphs and diagrams, stopwatch, pens, and numerous sheets covered with meticulously written mathematical signs and calculations. There is no piano in the room, nothing to intimate that it is a composer's workshop.

Karlheinz Stockhausen

"Essentially I am interested in pluralism," Stockhausen muses without looking at me. "In a multiple world of sound, with individual sounds and time relations, conflict must be solved in such a way that a condition is reached in which only something homogeneous and immutable is perceived. Do you see what I mean?"

He turns now to look at me with a severe expression. I am reluctant to admit that I do not understand him, but my expression gives me away. "You see," he continues, "for years we have been trying to create art all in one idiom, one style at one time. If you didn't abide by this axiom people would say, 'Ah, the métier is not consistent!' But why? Why should we not combine many things in one work of art?"

"In other words," I say with care, "in a work of yours like *Momente* you try to mix stylistic qualities, one after the other?"

"No, not entirely," he says with a trace of Germanic authority. "You are right, but you are also wrong. One after another, yes; but why not also at the same time? Why not a music which at one instance has operative potential on several levels?"

"Do you think," I ask, "that your interest in this kind of pluralism is somewhat responsible for the fact that you have been called a musical clown by some of your less admiring critics?"

He winces at my question. "A clown? Well, as I have said before, I must sometimes put up with being labeled a sensationalist, a composer out to create shock, even a cabaret clown, before understanding of the purely musical range of problems of tone-color composition sets in. The extramusical activities which I sometimes draw upon have nothing to do with external purposes. They develop out of purely musical criteria, as part of that organic process which differentiates music from mathematics. I am a product of many influences; naturally I draw upon them freely and sometimes unconsciously."

Stockhausen pauses momentarily, and then in an entirely different voice—one softened by vulnerability—he says: "My music makes sense to me. I can't ever understand why it is so difficult for other people."

Now there is a self-conscious pause. I try to fill the silence. "You have frequently mentioned Anton Webern during our conversations. You must feel a special indebtedness to his music."

"Ah, that is a very important subject: Webern, yes! You see, he condensed all music into what we call the needle's eye. Now, if you see what I mean, it has passed through the eye and is expanding in terms which are consistent with that condensation. Oh, yes, all music must start with Webern; there is no other choice!"

"And Stravinsky?" (At the time Stravinsky was still living.)

"Well, he is a very great man, of course, but he has not done very much in recent years."

"And American composers? Do you feel America has created any great composers?"

"Not really. John Cage is a very inventive gentleman with great bravery. But I'm not sure what it adds up to."

"How about Charles Ives?"

"Well, you have just rediscovered him here in America. For me he has been a great curiosity since I was a child. But as for his being a mainstream composer—no; like Kafka, he seems to be his own beginning, middle, and end."

"In the field of European music you are frequently linked with two of your close friends, Pierre Boulez and Luciano Berio."

Stockhausen is not overjoyed by the comparison. "That is correct," he says with restraint. "After the war, Pierre and I were working on very much the same problems. But soon we went off in our own directions."

"And Berio?"

"Luciano is Italian, Pierre Boulez is French, and I am German. Though I dislike making that kind of distinction, it is nonetheless unavoidable. For me *form* is everything. New form, of course, but form all the same! Perhaps Berio is more concerned with the emotional side of music. I'm not entirely certain. Boulez has something I don't have. He can rework the same piece for five years, always improving upon his own ideas, always changing a note, a measure. . . . From the needle's eye we have moved eons apart."

"Perhaps we can talk for a moment about *Momente* since it was your first major orchestral work released on records in the United States and has caused a greater controversy here than it did in Europe when it was premiered four years ago, in 1962. You've mentioned to me that most of the text of that work is drawn from letters written by you or sent to you by friends. I also understand that the formal scheme of *Momente*—I mean the 1965 performance diagram—draws its symbols from the names of people close to you: the K in the diagram refers to Karlheinz, the M refers to Mary Bauermeister, and so forth. Why do you tend to withhold this kind of information from the public?"

"What difference does it make? It does absolutely nothing to illuminate the music, and the music is the only thing I am concerned with."

"*Momente* is a very dramatic work. In view of your reputation as an ultramodernist, do you object to my saying that *Momente* has a strong romantic character?"

"No, no, of course not. But that is only part of it. It is also classi-

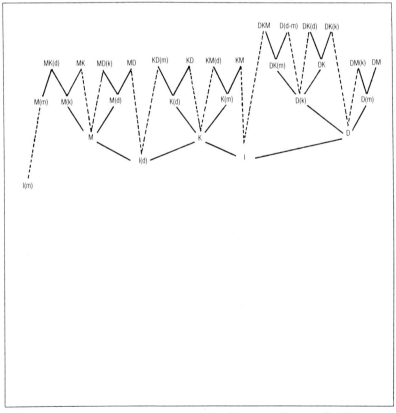

Performance diagram for Momente

cal and impressionistic and expressionist—all of these things, sometimes all at one time."

"Can such music possess point of view?"

"Since all art is the product of evaluation, all art automatically expresses point of view. You said that to me yourself not more than two days ago."

"What would you say is the major extramusical idea behind *Momente?*"

"Look," Stockhausen exclaims, leaning far out the window so that his hair is caught in the breeze, "that sailboat just capsized! You see, you never know what is going to happen next!"

In 1966, I had attended a performance of Stockhausen's *Kontakte* at the San Francisco Museum of Art. That's how we met. From that beginning, Stockhausen and I became friends. He visited The Contemporary Center and was touched by the range and daring of our activities. I explained that I wanted to use *Kontakte* as the basis for a dance composition, but before giving me permission to choreograph the piece, Stockhausen wanted to see my work. So one afternoon I set up a movie projector and dug out a couple of films of works I had created for the local PBS station. Soon Mary Bauermeister (a painter, who later married Stockhausen), Luciano Berio, and Stockhausen himself arrived, and I showed them the films. As a result, we presented Berio's *Visage* and Stockhausen's *Kontakte* as dance works.

My acquaintance with Stockhausen grew during the months he was a guest professor at the University of California at Davis. Eventually he suggested that we collaborate on a major project.

"For years Pierre Boulez and I have talked about a kind of musical performance in which action is an indigenous component," Stockhausen said. "We always talked about actors—Pierre and I—because musicians were not capable of the kind of action we wanted. But we never thought of dancers for some reason. Isn't that strange?" he mused, giving in to a boyish grin that he infrequently allowed to dart across his lips. Then, as abruptly, an expression of formality, almost an expression of disdain, came over his face.

It was the end of an eight-hour session in which Stockhausen and

I had discussed our plans. Somehow the hours had overtaken us. "My God, it's already three in the morning," I said.

"Well, it doesn't matter," he said. But then his concentration, which had been unfaltering for the entire evening, evaporated. He began to vanish into himself. It was an experience I had come to expect of him. It was always like that: we would talk breathlessly and with great enthusiasm, and then, quite abruptly, Stockhausen would seem to drift away into his own thoughts.

That evening was one of several meetings during which Stockhausen and I worked on the new theater piece. At one point I said, "What shall we call it? How about *Mimesis?*"

"No . . . no," Stockhausen muttered. "That sounds antique. This is something revolutionary that we're doing. This project must have a new kind of name—something almost religious without being religious, if you know what I mean. For ten years they have been calling my work 'points' and 'moments' and all kinds of things that suggest the science of immediacy. I think that's old-fashioned now. Now we need something new. A really new kind of name!"

As it turned out, the project was never completed. I had grown increasingly disenchanted with San Francisco. We had almost ceased performing or presenting other artists at The Contemporary Center. Instead we rented our theater to a company of actors that did standard commercial plays, and we had to do endless national tours in order to make enough money to survive as a dance company. Ironically, our tours turned out to be very successful, and though my work still perplexed and annoyed many people, at last we were getting the kind of audiences and reviews that we had always dreamed of having. San Francisco columnist Herb Caen summed up our situation with this item: "From a review by the toughest of critics, Claudia Cassidy in [the] *Chicago Tribune:* 'Thanks to you, San Francisco, for this superb dance company! The audience, which gave the dancers sixteen calls on the final curtain, had already reddened its hands from abundant applause for various individual dances. The lady next to me said, San Francisco must be quite a city to produce a company like this, and I agree.' The San Francisco Ballet? No [the] Contemporary Dancers of 1725 Washington Street, who, ironically, appear almost everywhere in the land EXCEPT San Francisco. Not enough financial support here. 'San Francisco must be quite a city. . . .' "

One day, while we were lumbering across America on a bus-and-truck tour, I suddenly recalled the advice of Anais Nin: "Go to New York!" Maybe she had always been right, I thought. In San Francisco we had been steadily ignored or attacked. Even the Actors Workshop was talking about relocating. Perhaps our kind of art could find a more supportive and enlightened public in New York. And so, while I gazed out the window of a Trailways bus and felt the terrible stupidity of having to give up ten years of effort, I decided to pack it up and start all over again.

At my next meeting with Stockhausen we forgot all about our work and discussed what kind of costume Stockhausen should wear to his farewell party, for his residency at the university was coming to an end. The last time I saw him in San Francisco was at a rather wild costume party on a houseboat in Sausalito, where his friends and students had gathered to wish him farewell. He was wearing an elegant gray kimono, looking very austere and stoical, even in the midst of the howling music of a local rock band.

For several years Stockhausen and I would be linked by letters about his music, his turbulent personal life, and our friendship. My library acquired numerous autographed copies of his new scores. And then, in 1971, when I saw him again at Lincoln Center, where the New York Philharmonic was premiering one of his compositions, we hardly recognized one another, for those were the days when almost everyone underwent drastic changes in appearance. I had shoulder-length black hair and a dozen strands of beads; while Stockhausen's cropped Germanic haircut had given way to long, flowing locks, and his very proper English suit and tie had been exchanged for a blouse and sport pants.

"Is it really you?" he exclaimed when I greeted him after the performance. Then we embraced and laughed. "Did you see!" he exclaimed. "They used your article about me in tonight's program!"

We looked at one another for a long time, and then Stockhausen said: "So now you are a writer! You see, it's just as I always said: you never know what is going to happen next!"

THE ROCK ERA
BEGINS

It is the night of November 6, 1965, in a loft in San Francisco. The atmosphere is luminous and wild: movie screens with flashing images like frenzied paintings hanging in midair, an overflowing crowd of undulating bodies in outrageous costumes, hair flying, eyes bedazzled, exuberant smiles amidst pungent smoke. There are several huge punch bowls filled with some mysterious new potion of the era. And in a corner six very young kids who call themselves the Jefferson Airplane are making a strange new music. Later that same night a few other musical novices will be heard for the first time: The Mystery Trend (soon to become the Great Society, with singer

Inside the Fillmore West

Grace Slick), the Warlocks (to become known as the Grateful Dead), an ensemble of street poets turned musicians called the Fugs, and the Charlatans.

This party has been organized by a fast-talking, aggressive, and very shrewd man from New York City named Bill Graham. He has been hanging around San Francisco for a few years, moving through the declining Beat scene, trying to figure out what he wants to do with his life.

Bill Graham was the producer of a theatrical group called the San Francisco Mime Troupe. At the time of the loft party, the Mime Troupe was just beginning to get involved in political ideas and street theater. "By late 1965," Graham later recounts, "we got to a point where we were really broke. Everybody in the Mime Troupe was living on about ninety-three cents a month. In November of 1965, exactly November sixth it was, I decided to hold this benefit for the Troupe."

The loft where that benefit took place comfortably held perhaps seven hundred people. But by midnight there were a thousand bodies jammed into the space. The whole company of San Francisco underground celebrities had turned out: Allen Ginsberg and Lawrence Ferlinghetti; filmmakers Bruce Baillie, Bruce Connor, and Bob Nelson; and actor Taylor Mead; dancers, painters, composers, musicians, and just about everybody else who was involved in the arts.

By one a.m. there was a line outside, with people pressing forward to get into the crowded loft. Then the police arrived and began telling people to leave. "Listen!" Graham cried out with that insane intensity of his, "you just can't close us down now. We've got Sinatra coming in at six, and we're expecting Belafonte! They're jetting in from Los Angeles!" Graham pleaded. "You just can't shut me down now!" But the tall tales didn't placate the authorities, who announced that if everyone did not leave the area they would call for the wagons.

"It was one of those unbelievable nights," Graham later recalled, smiling broadly, "and it didn't end up till maybe six in the morning with Ginsberg doing his chants ... it was really something else again!"

Bill Graham was a focal point of energy during the golden era of San Francisco rock music—the archpromoter and manager of the famed Fillmore Auditorium—a derelict theater in the black ghetto where, many years earlier, major black performers had made a sound that used to be called "race music" by people in the record business. But Graham was just one of several prime movers of the golden era. There was also the soft-spoken and thoroughly rural entrepreneur named Chet Helm who eventually headed a commune called the Family Dog and who organized another, equally famous rock palace called the Avalon Ballroom—a second-story hall on Sutter Street used by local social clubs for occasional Saturday night foxtrotting.

The Fillmore and the Avalon were highly competitive, and so Graham and Helm were not friends. There used to be a great deal of heated discussion in San Francisco about which of them was the real innovator on the rock scene. Clearly, Graham was the better promoter, whereas Chet Helm made his exceptional contributions and then faded away, never becoming a celebrity like Graham. Graham was not always liked by the people with whom he worked. On the other hand, Chet Helm was greatly respected as a gentle and "tribal" kind of person. Chet was utterly idealistic and truly devoted to the fragile hippie ideal of the period. Graham apparently saw that idealism in more practical terms.

There was a third person who helped organize and run the rock scene in the Bay Area. Berkeley was the territory dominated by Ed Denson and a group he managed called Country Joe and the Fish. "When Joe MacDonald moved up from Los Angeles," Denson told me, "he was publishing a magazine with protest tunes, poetry, drawings, and that sort of thing. That was about the middle of 1965. I was just about to start a folk-song magazine myself, so we got together on the project. What happened was that the magazine wasn't really concerned with folk music at all. Instead we did things like "Fixin' to Die," and "The LSD Rag," and people were really excited about the tunes we printed. So we decided to put out a single record. It was a little single that we recorded in a living room so it could be used as part of the October peace demonstration in Berkeley."

The scene in Berkeley, though only fifteen minutes by car from San Francisco, was completely different from the Haight-Ashbury

Country Joe MacDonald

world of hippies. "For instance," Denson explained, "though I've never really figured it out, Bill Graham did a pretty good job of ignoring anything that happened in Berkeley. Ultimately, Graham was right in refusing to hire nonprofessional musicians. He did hire Country Joe and the Fish a couple of times for the Fillmore, but on the whole he imported blues bands. At that time, Graham was trying to decide whether or not to be a hippie. He must have decided against it, because he stopped hiring the hip bands for a long while; he stopped using us and he stopped using Big Brother and the Holding Company and the Quicksilver Messenger Service. All for the same reason, I guess: because when you come down to it, though the hip bands really made a good noise and really turned on the kids, they really didn't perform very well in terms of professional standards."

Prior to 1967, when San Francisco moved into the foregound of the international rock picture, the Berkeley sound, as it was called, was essentially devoted to "peacenik" music—tunes expressing strong political views—whereas the San Francisco sound was "the tribal music of the hippies," songs closely related to the various drug experiences that had become social issues in California. County Joe MacDonald was identified with Berkeley, while the Jefferson Airplane and Big Brother and the Holding Company were two of the major bands identified with San Francisco.

The Jefferson Airplane was the first of the local bands to have a commercial recording released, by RCA Victor. "Before the Airplane's big success," Denson told me, "we didn't have any of the commercial and record-industry interests sniffing around the Bay Area. But by the time the Grateful Dead's album was issued, everybody was looking at San Francisco to see if the Airplane was just a unique hit or if there was really a scene going on here. We made our first LP at just the right moment: before the superhype and just after the Airplane gave the city a lot of attention."

I had a front seat during the rise of the San Francisco rock scene. The Airplane's erratic manager, Matthew Katz, had his office at The Contemporary Center, and he arranged to have the Airplane's first promotional photographs taken in front of our theater. The group called Moby Grape was also a tenant. At this time I was starting to work with progressive jazz and gospel and rock music—to the considerable consternation of many of my creative associates—and I had become especially friendly with Chet Helm and Peter Albin of Big Brother and the Holding Company. Many of us knew that something exceptional was taking place in San Francisco. I remember being at a party with the poet Kenneth Rexroth. It must have been about the middle of 1965, and I recall his saying that Grant Avenue where the Beats hung out was finished and that the new place was going to be Haight-Ashbury. But at the time, it seemed unlikely that San Francisco would ever become a popular-music capital. The Beatles were well into in their so-called middle period, and the Rolling Stones were just beginning to become well known. The Byrds were starting up in Los Angeles, although their sound at the time was far closer to folk music than to rhythm and blues. The Sunset Strip in Los Angeles, which would soon become a mecca for every kind of crazy person in the world, was still an elegant row of restaurants and nightclubs. The first clear sign that something unusual was happening in San Francisco was the benefit party for the Mime Troupe.

"The first benefit which Graham presented was actually done at the suggestion of the Family Dog," Chet Helm insisted. "It was the most electrifying event that had ever happened. In any case, I think there was this sort of sudden realization that the fuzz just couldn't bust us *all* at one time. Twelve hundred people! I mean, prior to that time—honest to God—there wasn't one of those people at that dance who didn't go through mortal terror every day just walking down a street with long hair and that sort of thing. Because San Francisco was a very tight scene, as you well know. Tight as any little town in America. It's only in the last two or three years that it's really loosened up because we've brought about a cultural coup to the city in posters, in environmental design, underground newspapers, and—of course—the music and what the music says."

"San Francisco was the forerunner of everything we now associate with the 1960s youth movement," Ed Denson told me back in January of 1968, when I had already moved to New York but was back in the Bay Area to research a book. "True, the Los Angeles *Free Press* is very big now, but it took most of its form from the *Berkeley Barb* and the *San Francisco Oracle* and all the years and years of effort that had gone into underground magazines and papers in San Francisco long before Los Angeles was much more than a movie capital. After the media started making a big thing of San Francisco, you could see the youth impulse spreading everywhere."

At about the time Chet Helm and Wes Wilson began to produce the series of "psychedelic" posters that became a trademark of the youth movement, many young people were beginning to make radical changes in their appearance and dress: bright colors, beads and bells, long hair, beards, and bare feet. Many San Franciscans took one look at what was going on and had the vapors. "I can remember a time," Chet recalled, "when George Hunter of the Charlatans used to walk into a party where everybody was listening to classical music, because that was the big San Francisco elegant number at the time . . . and he would put on the Rolling Stones or the Beatles or the Kinks or something of that order. I mean, we had to spirit that cat out of a number of parties. I think George Hunter was one of the very first great 'heads.' He was really something else! As for Graham—I've got to say on his behalf that he's been very valuable in respect to his initial hassles with the city fathers. . . . I'm going through the same things in Denver, where I just opened a rock club. It's really rough, and it's given me a lot more respect for Graham."

When Graham was confronted by these remarks in 1968, he smiled without much pleasure. "But we live in the United States of America, and everything that succeeds succeeds like all hell and some. The kids made San Francisco into an international hip capital. Many of them resent it now because it has changed the scene so much and has made it pretty artificial; but it did something to San Francisco: it turned the city on! And that's something!" As for his differences of opinion with Chet Helm: "Now, there may have been some dances before my party at the loft, but all I know is that that dance was the first one to really make it big. I wasn't in the business of running parties or dances. I was just putting on a theater hustle to raise some bread for the Mime Troupe. You see? Well, I was living on Twenty-fifth Avenue at the time, and I used to drive home down Geary Boulevard. And I used to look at the old Fillmore Auditorium . . . years before, it had been a skating rink, but in the last ten or fifteen years they had used it for blues shows for the local black population. On December eighth of 1965—and I really remember that date—I looked at the place and the owner said he'd let me have it for a Saturday night for sixty dollars. Well, that was the first dance concert .. while the loft was just a party where everybody got stoned and had a good time. This time there was lots of room, and there was dancing and we showed films and slides and it was a huge success. So December tenth was the first Fillmore dance concert. And, you see, I had already left the Mime Troupe, and my head began to put some pieces together and I realized that there was something happening in San Francisco and the rock scene was it! So I held a second dance at the Fillmore on January fourteenth of 1966. Then I realized that I had to talk the owner of the auditorium into leasing the place to me. It was a big hassle, and I won't go into it, but anyway, by the end of January, I had the place signed and I started making plans for its use. I was still very big on cheesebox [experimental] theater—I'd give everything up even now to get back to it—so I originally thought I'd use the Fillmore as both a theater and a rock dance hall. Anyway, right after I signed the lease with the landlord, I allowed Ken Kesey, who actually started the whole freak-out scene—I allowed Ken to go into the auditorium with a production which I presented on January twenty-first, twenty-second, and twenty-third of 1966. That really blew the lid off the whole scene. That's where all the groovy words came from. Then I knew that San Francisco had taken it much further than London or anywhere else. I knew that something really powerful was beginning to happen. I didn't know how I had gotten into the middle of it, but I knew I was there!"

Eventually the Fillmore moved to a new location, and Graham, who had bought the old building, donated it to the black community. The Fillmore that the youthful pilgrims of the summer of 1967 saw when they came to San Francisco with flowers in their hair was not the Fillmore that I remembered. Chet Helm thought that Graham ran his concerts with too much restriction. "That's the trouble with the old whiskey bars," Chet complained, "they were never really permissive. Maybe Bill isn't really into this scene; I am, and I understand what's happening and what you must permit if people are going to be their best. Also, there's another difference: I'm part of the tribe and I really dig the music."

"I'm a New Yorker," Bill Graham retorted without apology, "and I love Afro and Cuban music. Latin and Brazilian stuff with a beat, you know. As for rock, I wasn't then and I'm not now that insane about the music. I like rhythm and blues much better than rock. But what I did like is what I saw rock did for people. That was beautiful!"

"Anyway," Ed Denson said in an effort to provide a summary of the conflicting histories I had heard during my research, "there was the big fight between Graham and the Family Dog [Chet Helm] which we don't need to go into in any detail. The fact is that Chet approached Bill to suggest that their two organizations join efforts, and Bill said that he didn't want any partners."

Chet and Bill did collaboratively present the first Paul Butterfield Blues Band concert at the Fillmore before it had become a rock palace. After the concert, Graham recalled, "we went into the office and we had all these boxes of money. You see we had none of us ever really made any big money before and we weren't in any way prepared for what happened. So when the hundreds and hundreds of dollars started coming in, we just shoved the money into boxes. Well, we sat on the floor and we dumped all this bread in a pile and we just sat there looking at it."

"We've got to book Butterfield again real soon!" Chet and Bill agreed.

The bad blood between Graham and Helm seems to have developed out of that situation. The gist of the matter is that Bill got up early, and the early bird got Paul Butterfield for a return concert. Chet felt cheated. "I was pretty naive about business," he later admitted to me. For a time, Chet and Bill continued using the Fillmore on alternate weekends, because neither of them had enough capital at the time to finance the whole undertaking. Eventually Bill got the lease on the building, and Chet was out.

After Chet Helm left the Fillmore, he searched for a rock palace of his own. That's where he and I got involved. During 1966, I had created a show called *Blast!* that used six or seven old-guard jazzmen as well as Big Brother and the Holding Company. It was a very experimental effort, using theater, projections, lights, dance, and music. Ralph Gleason hated it and Phillip Elwood loved it—and they were the music monarchs of the local press. But despite good and bad reviews, people in San Francisco weren't ready for a sit-down rock production. Musical events in those days were still presented in big empty dance halls without seating, so people could listen and dance at the same time. So *Blast!* played to an audience consisting almost entirely of musicians for six or eight weekends and then slipped away into oblivion.

We had a party after the opening night of *Blast!*, and many people in the music scene turned up. Among them was Matthew Katz (the manager of the Airplane), Chet, and attorney Sam Ridge, as well as jazz musician Virgil Gonzalves. Just as Graham had frequently passed the Fillmore and thought about making it into a rock palace, so, too, had I often passed the old Avalon Ballroom, located a couple of blocks from the basement where I lived when I first arrived in San Francisco and was teaching modern dance at a tap-dance studio. I don't remember exactly how it happened, but in the course of a conversation about the Fillmore, I mentioned the Avalon. Sam Ridge and Virgil Gonzalves, Matthew Katz, and Chet Helm decided to look into the Avalon. The next thing I heard about the Avalon was that Sam and Virgil had been outbid and that the Family Dog and Chet were taking it over. A few years later, when I returned to San Francisco, I sat with Janis Joplin at the enormously popular Avalon, wondering how the music scene had become so complex. By now Graham had another Fillmore on Second Avenue in New York City. I remember I went there to see a concert a few weeks after a book of mine, *Rock and Other Four Letter Words,* had been published. Bill, who had always been reasonably nice to me, stormed up in full sail, guns blasting, shouting over the blast of music coming from the stage. He utterly hated my book . . . told me it was nothing but a lot of nonsense. A few days later, Richard Kostelanetz, in *The New York Times Book Review,* called it "one of the most inventively conceived books of the decade."

For those of us who were part of the popular music scene back in 1965 to 1967, the golden era of rock in San Francisco was both a marvelous and shattering experience. I continued to write about pop music for another three years, because I believed that the music was part of a vital new idealism that had emerged in an otherwise repressive and conservative America. Yet I never felt that I was truly part of the pop world, for my major interests lay elsewhere. I remember one night when I was sitting with Linda Eastman and a journalist from Australia named Lillian Roxon in the back room at Max's Kansas City, Lillian told me I was "just passing through the pop scene." I think she rather resented it.

For those of us who saw it happen from the front row, it was far more than a "scene." People we knew became instant celebrities. Many of them also died. Ed Denson probably understood the situation better than most of us. "Berkeley," he recalls, "started the international student-activist movement. Country Joe and I were part of that impulse. San Francisco started the hippie movement. Soon the activists and the hippies intermixed; we were political, then we were hippies, and then we drifted back to activism again. The activists believed that effort will bring results; the hippies, on the whole, felt that no amount of effort will rectify the mess the world is in. The 'doing your own thing' concept is a resolution for living in a world where united effort doesn't improve the human situation."

The golden era of rock has faded so utterly and has been so strongly criticized for its excesses that we have forgotten some of the ideals and hopes that came out of it. Today, the attitude of the young has changed so drastically from the views of both activists and hippies that it sometimes seems as if the 1960s never took place. Like all periods of great change and upheaval, it may take a good deal of time and reflection before we can recognize what really happened to all of us during that brilliant and tragic era.

NEW YORK CITY: THE ROCK ERA CONTINUES

I was exalted and terrified by New York City. Having spent most of my life in the West, I was utterly unprepared for the turmoil of the city. In 1967, I leaped directly out of San Francisco's so-called Summer of Love into a sultry and staggeringly aggressive Manhattan August. The Lower East Side of New York was a combat zone by comparison to the naive friendliness of Haight-Ashbury. It took very little time for me to realize that a person could get his brains bashed at the corner of St. Marks Place and Second Avenue. I could not deal with the immense amount of debris and the corruption. I was appalled by the lines of derelict buildings. I was astonished by the bodies passed out on the pavements and by the nonchalance of the people stepping over them. The poverty was so harsh and visible that I immediately realized that you were dead in New York if you didn't have money.

I didn't have any money.

I sublet an actor's apartment in the most deranged part of the Village, on MacDougal Street. The actor was away on a six-month tour, and so I thought I would have plenty of time to get some kind of work and find a place of my own. Wrong. Suddenly the actor reenters. His six-month tour has been cancelled after only six weeks. "You'll have to move," he tells me, without the slightest concern for our agreement that I would have the place for six months. I strongly object, but he tells me to pack my things and be gone by the end of the week. That's New York!

I remembered a hotel where Jamie Herlihy had stayed when he first arrived in New York. I called Jamie and he asked me to dinner at his flat on East 7th Street. When I finally located his building I was astonished by its miserable state. I was totally unaware of the living conditions in Manhattan. Though I would never have admitted it then, the fact of the matter was that I had grown up in the fabled opulence of western suburbia. Garbage and soot and filth were strangers to me. Though I had been poor, I had never lived in poverty. New York offered no sanctuary from pain and hunger.

As I climbed to the fifth floor ("Where is the elevator?") and knocked at Jamie's door, my spirits sank. Surely a published writer like Herlihy didn't have to live like this in New York.

When Jamie opened his door, I suddenly discovered the other Manhattan—the one that exists behind the derelict facades. Abruptly the world changed. Jamie's apartment floated above the filth and gloom: gleaming white walls, posters and paintings, candles burning on ledges and tables, plants filling the incensed air. It was like the interior of those mirrors through which Jean Cocteau voyaged. Once you plunged through the surface of New York, you found yourself in an inner sanctum where people used imagination and ingenuity to transform hovels into places to live.

Herlihy and I had a delicious dinner, which he managed to produce in a minuscule kitchen. We talked about all the years since we had last seen each other in Los Angeles. And we talked about what I hoped to do with my life now that I was finally in New York.

"If you want to write," Jamie explained, "you'll have to have some connections. I've found it almost impossible to make a living writing. And if you want to continue in dance, you'll need dancers and a place to work. It's a tough town," he said.

"Right now I need to find a place to live," I explained. He offered to share his tiny flat, but I knew that I needed a place of my own. So I asked him about the hotel where he had stayed when he had arrived in New York without any money. "Well," he cautioned, "it was never paradise, and it's gotten a good deal worse since I stayed there. But here's the address."

The hotel was located on Washington Square and had long been a haven for people in the arts. Indeed, it had gone downhill considerably since Herlihy had lived there. But at least it was a place to stay until I could locate an apartment.

The apartment I eventually found was located south of Houston Street on the edge of Little Italy. The neighborhood was easily the worst I had seen in New York. As I climbed the stairs with the agent, elderly people peered out at me and grunted or screamed incomprehensible messages to neighbors on the floors above and below them. The apartment itself had been the home of a woman for forty years. She had died two weeks earlier, and the landlord was still dragging her pitiful belongings away. The plaster was falling from the ceiling and the walls were battered and filthy. A frail light came in from the gray windows. Rat droppings covered the floors, and hundreds of roaches scrabbled into the walls when I opened the cabinets. There was a rusty old bathtub in the middle of the kitchen. And still on the wall was a stained embroidery in a broken frame, greeting me with a ridiculous message: "Home, Sweet Home."

The rent was thirty-six dollars a month. And recalling what Herlihy had done with his apartment, I decided to sign a lease. Twenty years later I still have that rent-controlled apartment. But the neighborhood has drastically changed. It is now among the most fashionable districts in Manhattan, and my neighbors are paying six times more rent for their decontrolled apartments than I pay for mine. But that's the price you pay to live in Soho.

It has always been the high energy of New York that has attracted me. It is the city's daring and permissiveness and willingness to assimilate vast numbers of diversified people that make it both a great metropolis and a horrendous slum. In New York, people are such scoundrels that they accept a little bit of the scoundrel in everyone. It is one of the few great cities of the world in which a person of achievement is not required to be respectable. And since you can't be an achiever in the arts and be respectable, New York's tolerance makes it possible for people to dream themselves and their incredible schemes and ideas into existence.

Five weeks after arriving in New York City, I was sitting in the Sutton Place apartment of John Waxman, talking about what I wanted to do with my life. I knew John through his illustrious father, the film composer Franz Waxman, with whom I had collaborated on a theater piece. John was an executive at Bantam Books, and when he asked me why I didn't supplement my work in theater by using my skill as a writer to produce books, I leaped at the opportunity without having given it any previous thought. "What kind of book could you do for us?" he asked. I didn't have the slightest idea. But out of my desperation to survive in New York and out of that dark place in us where ideas are born, something came flying out of my mouth before I really knew what I was saying. "I'd like to do a very original book about the rock scene. Not just a book for adolescent fans, but a really inventive portrait of what I saw in San Francisco."

"And what would you call it?" John asked.

Again the words poured out of me: "How about calling it *Rock and Other Four Letter Words?*"

"I like it," he said.

A week later I had a contract to do my first book. I also had an advance that represented more money than I had ever had at one time in my entire life.

That's New York!

BRIEFLY
LINDA EASTMAN

For days after signing the contract to write *Rock and Other Four Letter Words* I walked around in a glow, utterly insulated from the madness of New York City. Then I suddenly realized that I didn't have any idea how to write such a book.

I spent a month going from one record company to the next, talking to anyone who might provide the connections I would need to get involved in the local pop scene.

"A book about rock 'n' roll?" executives and press agents asked incredulously. "Who will want to read a book about rock 'n' roll?"

This was 1967, the era of teenybopper fan magazines and hysterical

Linda Eastman

disc jockeys. And though I looked like a hippie, I much preferred Stockhausen to Elvis Presley.

My luck finally changed when I met Danny Fields, a considerable force in the New York rock world and the "house hippie" at Elektra Records. He offered to play Virgil to my Dante, conducting me through the rings of Hell: Max's Kansas City, The Scene, the Anderson Theater (which long predated Graham's Fillmore East), and every other hot spot where rock musicians and their legions of groupies spent the late hours.

One night, Danny took me to a concert by The Who at the Old Village Theater. In the lobby he absently introduced me to a woman named Linda Eastman. Then, typically, he walked off with friends and left me standing there. I glanced uncomfortably at Linda. She had a Nikon camera strapped over each shoulder and was carrying a huge and very old brown leather purse. I learned much later that her brother John had only recently brought the Nikons for her from Japan. It seems that she was as inexperienced as a pop photographer as I was as a pop journalist.

"Hear you're doing a book on rock," she said as she collected her belongings and shoved them into her enormous purse. "Need a photographer?"

Just as I was about to respond, a cascade of little metal film cans tumbled from her purse and scattered over the lobby carpet. I joined her on my hands and knees to help collect them. I took the opportunity to scrutinize her curiously interesting face—without a trace of makeup and with very soft blue eyes.

"Call me sometime so we can talk. Okay?" she said.

"Okay."

During the next couple of weeks I talked to several photographers who regularly covered the rock scene for various record companies and underground newspapers. Most of them produced rather standard, uninteresting publicity shots. So eventually I invited myself over to Linda's apartment in the east eighties so I could see her photographs. Her daughter, Heather, smiled up at me while I gazed around. The walls were papered with pictures. I was instantly impressed by the awkwardness, innocence, and candor of her photographs. You could tell from them that she loved both the music and the people who made it.

"What do you think?" she asked.

"I like them."

"Well, how about your book?"

"I need to think about it," I replied.

The next week, a publicist suggested that I interview the Beach Boys at a nearby suburban college where they were playing a one-night stand. I called Linda: "I don't want to feel committed, so let's just say you can come along if you want to take some pictures."

When we got to the auditorium, there was general chaos at the box office. In those days, there was no special provision made for the press, and Linda and I had to wait on line. Finally, when I got to the window, I announced that press tickets had been left for us.

"Sorry, no one left your name."

"Well, I . . ."

"Next!"

Since I couldn't get through to the person in the box office, we decided to wander toward the back of the building. Eventually we spotted an unguarded door and slipped in. The next problem was finding our way backstage, which proved to be particularly difficult insofar as a very large woman was guarding the stage door. Linda diverted her attention by taking her photograph, while I sneaked backstage and hurried into the first dressing room I found. I landed in the midst of the Beach Boys, who were busily brushing their white jackets. "Hi," one of them said pleasantly.

I introduced myself and explained that I was doing a book and wondered if I could plug in my tape recorder and interview them.

"Right now we're trying to get ready for our set, but if you'll wait we can give you some time just before we go on."

I wandered out into the hall, where Linda was talking to a musician. A band was on stage, blasting away, and I couldn't hear anything she said to me. The frenzy backstage was staggering, but Linda seemed totally at ease.

Flocks of girls, like molting birds with feathers flying, took off in clusters as they were chased up and down the halls by private policemen. For a moment the girls would vanish, only to reappear and cautiously peek through doors and around corners, hoping to catch sight of a superstar. Then the policemen would come back and the birds would scatter once again.

We didn't even get to hear the Beach Boys perform. A policeman approached us as we were settling in the wings to listen. "You can't stand there. What are you doing back here, anyway?"

Linda and I gave each other an exasperated glance and walked out the stage door, where several journalists were arguing nobly, trying to be admitted.

The next time I saw Linda was at a recording session in midtown Manhattan. Cream was cutting a record. We were admitted to the control booth. Through the thick glass partition we could see four musicians hunched over their instruments in the eerie glow of a single red spotlight: drummer Ginger Baker with his wild crown of fuzzy hair, lead guitarist Eric Clapton, and bass guitarist Jack Bruce, along with Felix Pappalardi, their young producer, sitting in at the organ. The music was surprisingly more complex and polished than anything else I had heard in the rock scene. These were musicians with a good deal of experience in jazz.

We were hearing the birth of a tune called "Passing the Time," which was eventually released on Cream's third album, *Wheels of Fire.*

A week later I finally made up my mind about Linda and gave her a call. "How about it—do you want to do some pictures for my book?" I asked.

She seemed neither surprised nor delighted by my offer.

Her attorney brother put together an agreement, and then we made our travel plans.

We decided that we would first go to London—since in 1967 that was where the pop scene was still concentrated. Then we would continue on to Los Angeles and San Francisco before returning to New York. I made a dozen long-distance calls, trying to set up interviews with British rock stars.

In London we stayed at the Cumberland Hotel, which stands at the edge of Hyde Park on Oxford Street. We produced a mild British sensation during our stay by having Jimmy Page for lunch and

Eric Clapton for tea. Page took us to a then-popular club, The Speak-easy, where we heard Pink Floyd—a band that Linda detested and I admired. We met Jimi Hendrix at the office of his promoter on Oxford Street, just down from the hotel. He was exasperatingly unco-operative, yawning and tapping his fingers on my tape recorder. It must have been a bad day for Hendrix: during all our subsequent meetings with him he was exceptionally polite and articulate.

The next day we traveled to Aston Tirrold—a town about forty miles from London, where a newly formed group called Traffic lived in a small collage. At the time Traffic consisted of Stevie Winwood, Jim Capaldi, Chris Wood, and Dave Mason. They had bought a huge four-track recorder and built a studio so they could lay down tracks in the seclusion of their cottage. We heard some of the takes for what would eventually become "Pearly Queen." Then Stevie sat down at the organ in the living room and began to sing a new tune, "Who Knows What Tomorrow May Bring." The afternoon had quickly vanished and it was already getting dark, but Linda was un-willing to budge. Unfortunately, I lost my sense of humor and hung around outside having a snit while she said her interminable good-byes. It was never easy to separate Linda from rock musicians, even when it was time to leave London and fly to the Pacific coast.

In San Francisco, the interview with the Grateful Dead was a free-for-all, with Jerry Garcia trying to make a bit of sense while the other musicians clowned. The Dead worked out of a vast white Vic-torian house in Haight-Ashbury, and during our visit various people kept running through the room and cherry bombs kept exploding. Linda looked impatient and irritated, and I couldn't much blame her. We had come to expect the kind of cordial treatment we had gotten from the English pop groups. Finally it was time for Linda to take pictures. She asked the group to assemble on the steps in front of the house, since she wanted something that would look like a Vic-torian family portrait. Bob Weir had found some "skiing equip-ment," and soon the members of the Grateful Dead were slowly "skiing" down the steps toward Linda. She stood her ground and kept taking pictures, resulting in one of the best sequences of pho-tographs in *Rock and Other Four Letter Words*.

On Sunday morning at ten sharp, my old friends of Big Brother and the Holding Company—Peter Albin, Sam Andrews, Janis Joplin, James Gurley, and Dave Getz—came to my hotel room. We talked for a long time, and then Linda and the fellows went down to Geary Boulevard to take some photographs.

Janis stayed to talk about her career as a singer. "I'm a chick singer and that's all I am," she said. "One day I am a beatnik and the next day I'm in all the magazines. I think it's great to be famous, but it's also a little scary."

When I asked her about her recent performances at the Monterey pop festival, she really smiled. "I couldn't sleep for several nights after it—I was so turned on. It was just unbelievable how great everything and everybody was to me. It's like the supreme experience. It's a reciprocal emotional and physical experience. And that's the whole way I correlate my music with everyday experience. It's completely separate from thought. When an audience is really with you, it's not thinking. It's just following a groove." And then Janis laughed her big, joyful laughter. "I think I have a good voice," she said. "What I'm learning is taste. I'm also learning more and more about my voice and how I can affect people with it. I learn every time I sing a song. I've done 'Ball and Chain' thousands of times—right? And just last week, I did a little new thing on one verse. And every time you do a new thing you notice whether it does or doesn't work. Every time I sing a song it grows a little bit and so do I."

Linda returned and Janis asked to be photographed in her favorite fur hat. She was so proud of that hat. I remember her beaming with confidence and pride as Linda took her picture. That was the last time I saw Janis.

During our long trip, Linda and I met and interviewed and photographed almost all the major rock stars of the period. We even managed to visit the elusive Beach Boys at Brian Wilson's extravagant Bel Air mansion. Then, in late January, we packed it up and flew back to New York. Linda processed and printed her photographs, eventually providing me with a huge stack of eight-by-tens. Then I said good-bye to her, for it was time for me to write and design the book.

Linda and I had traveled halfway around the world. We spent Christmas and New Year's Eve of 1967 together. We ate three meals a day together for four or five weeks. But we never became friends, and we seemed to have few common interests.

I have no idea what she thought of *Rock and Other Four Letter Words*. She didn't say and I didn't ask. Shortly after the book was released Linda married Paul McCartney.

CONVERSATION WITH
GEORGE MARTIN

George Martin looks like an English barrister. Actually he is responsible for some of the most successful recordings in the history of popular music. As musical mentor and record producer of the Beatles for many years, he was responsible for creating many of the innovative and trend-setting techniques of rock.

In the fall of 1968, when I talked to him, no one fully understood where Martin's creativity ended and the Beatles' talents began. In fact, Martin usually declined to talk about his role in the musical career of the Beatles. I suspect that my strong interest in classical music of the Baroque—a subject dear to George Martin—was the

George Martin

basis upon which he decided to grant me an interview. It wasn't modesty that prompted Martin's low profile, but his awareness that stardom often brings more pain than joy and more scandal than fame. "I rather trust," he said, "that you will treat me like a person who creates music and not like a pop star."

After attending the Guildhall School in London, where he majored in composition and minored in conducting and oboe, George Martin went to work for EMI, one of the world's largest record companies. It was November of 1950, and he started by recording classical music for Parlophone (a poor relation of EMI). By 1955 he had been put in charge of running EMI. He also produced some jazz records—among them, records by Humphrey Lyttleton and Johnny Dankworth.

Before working with the Beatles, George Martin had been recording the Goons's albums. The Goons—Peter Sellers, Spike Milligan, and Harry Secombe—had a popular radio series in England in the fifties. The show was a "very zany, slapstick sort of affair, if you understand," Martin told me. "The Beatles were great fans of the Goons and had seen my name listed as their record producer. So they were prepared to like me. I think that was an advantage in our getting along so well during the first sessions."

I asked what events led up to his meeting the Beatles.

"Syd Coleman was the managing director of the publishing company which EMI controlled, and he had offices in Oxford Street over the record shop which EMI owned there. Also in this record shop there were facilities for dubbing—you know, where one could have records made from tapes. Apparently Brian Epstein, who was the Beatles' manager, went along to the shop because he had some tapes of the boys that he wanted pressed as demonstration records. Well, the engineer thought they were interesting and talked to Syd Coleman on the telephone. Consequently, Coleman heard the tapes and also heard Brian Epstein's story—which was something of a hard-luck tale because he was not doing very well in getting the boys a record contract. Syd Coleman suggested to Brian that he bring the tapes around to me, because he knew I was on the lookout for anything odd. I had that reputation, as it were. Well, Brian came to see me and I gave a listen to the tapes and I thought they were interesting. Later I learned that Brian was at the end of his tether, having tried just about everybody in an effort to get the boys a record date. The people at Decca had told him, 'The boys won't go, Mr. Epstein. We know about these things. You have a good record business in Liverpool. Stick to it,' they told him."

Today it is very difficult to understand the exceptional insight and imagination it must have taken to appreciate the potential of the Beatles when listening to those early tapes for the first time. "As a record executive," I asked, "how did you manage to recognize their promise. What did they sound like?"

"The music was rough and it was very amateurish, indeed. In fact, I really don't blame anybody for having turned down those tapes which Brian had played for most of the record companies. They weren't at all good. I can't pretend that I even slightly anticipated the fame and power which the Beatles would win. I can't even say that I was particularly fond of the so-called Merseyside groups that were popular in England at the time. For instance, I had not particularly liked Shadow, a group that preceded the Beatles. I suppose the thing that intrigued me about them was that I was puzzled. There was one thing in the music that I couldn't account for, something that I wanted to find out more about. I think that's all I can really say about the day early in April of 1962 when I first heard the Beatles' tapes. I said to Brian on that day, 'Well, I can't make up my mind—but bring them down to London and I'll test them in the studio."

"At that time the Beatles were in Liverpool, is that right? And they were very disappointed by the constant rejection of their tapes by various record companies."

"I knew nothing about that, of course," George Martin said with a bit of irony in his voice. "Brian naturally spoke with enthusiasm about the boys and expressed his belief that they were England's answers to Elvis Presley. That sort of thing. Yes . . . the boys were in Liverpool."

"What was your impression when you first saw them? Their sort of look, which is so prominent all over London today, was hardly in vogue in 1962. Were the Beatles still in those leather getups they used in Hamburg, or had they changed? Did they slick up in order to make a conventional impression on you, or did they pretty much come as they were?"

"Well, frankly, I can't remember how they were dressed," Martin laughed. "I guess I should recall that day better than I do—but to me it was just another studio test. I recall thinking to myself that they had an exceptional mass of hair. And they wanted to give a very casual impression—they were pretty ungroomed by London standards. But I could certainly tell that they were very nervous and anxious. But what most impressed me about them was that they were very friendly and that they were very prevalent now, but at that time it was not the traditional kind of behavior for young men. I was impressed by their openness and optimism. They also had an odd sense of humor which very much suited me. As it turned out, the boys were tremendous fans of the Goons, so we shared the same appreciation for the absurd."

"I suppose the Beatles invented the glib humor that has become the hallmark of the whole rock scene," I suggested.

"Well, oddly enough, you are seeing something that really doesn't exist. That kind of banter generally existed only at press conferences and when the boys were on show. It's really a nervous reaction more than anything else. When they're privately involved with other people, they don't go around wisecracking. They're very ordinary people."

"Ringo wasn't with the group at that point, was he?"

"That's quite right. There was a drummer by the name of Pete Best, who came down with them from Liverpool. After the first recording session I sat down and listened to the tapes. Something was wrong. The drumming wasn't right. And besides, the guy didn't seem to fit in with the other Beatles. Oddly enough, I thought at the time that he was the best-looking in the group, but he was sort of mean, moody, and magnificent—like an American, if you know what I mean. He was the Marlon Brando of the four, which was just a bit comical. He was the guy who sat in the corner playing his drums without really joining in when the rest of the boys were in another part of the studio trying to make music. The things didn't jell at all. He didn't contribute any drive to the beat. And he seemed to be a loner. All of that is very fanciful stuff today because rock groups have mistakenly imitated stances of the Beatles which simply don't exist. They were performers and entertainers with a real interest in their audience. If anything, their first recordings were too much like performances—the boys really tried to put some guts into their playing. That's very rare in record sessions. The very fact that they were polite and anxious to please is what made Pete Best so unsuited to the rest of them. He seemed to have an ax to grind. Now, I didn't know that they were sort of feeling this way, too. They had already decided to change drummers, but Brian had asked them to wait because he was a little afraid of changing the image of the group at such a critical time, when they were very successful in the cellar clubs of Liverpool and were finally getting a record company audition. As for me, I wasn't just being critical and saying that this thing wasn't going to happen unless we got some good drumming.

"As I recall, I told Brian that I wasn't trying to influence what he was doing as a manager, but as far as a record was concerned, I was definitely going to get a studio drummer to do the drumming. You know, what I had in mind was a session musician with lots of professional experience. And Pete Best would have to go.

"Well, the drummer we found was Andy White. But Ringo Starr was also involved in those sessions. In fact, on the very first album, Ringo played maracas and Andy White played drums on 'Love Me Do.' On the single we released of that same tune—which is a totally different version, you know—Ringo played drums. We did the different single version because the boys wanted very much to remake it with Ringo because he was now a full-fledged member of the group. So I let them rerecord it."

"How did you happen to have two drummers for the session?"

"It was a lack of communication between Brian and the boys and me. I had told Brian that I would get a session drummer, and naturally I expected him to tell the boys about my plan. Meanwhile, the boys had been looking for another drummer. They found Ringo, and when Ringo came into the studio, he found Andy White, this session drummer, and he was rather bitter about it."

"What were the first recording sessions like? The Beatles were essentially amateurs as far as recording was concerned. . . ."

"No, they had recorded before. In fact, it was their German records that had first made Brian Epstein aware of them. The youngsters used to ask Brian for Beatles records at his Liverpool record shop. They had worked in Germany with Bert Kaempfert. But they were pretty raw and rough people. After the first record—which was 'Love Me Do' and 'P.S. I Love You'—well, I was pretty certain that I had a hit group on my hands. But I still wasn't sure about the material—the tunes, I mean. I knew they needed a hit song, but I wasn't convinced they could write it because everything they had written up to that time wasn't very good. The songs had beginnings, but nothing was really carried through successfully."

"In that period—1962—was it very usual for singers to come in with tunes of their own?" I asked.

"That's a good point, because so few people today realize how the record industry has changed. No, indeed, in those days it was very much a case of having a singer and trying to find a song and a good arrangement for him. You got songwriters to write songs or you went around to the publishers and tried to find a tune that would fit the singer. In those days, we totally tailored a commercial product: arrangements, promotion, tunes, biography, all that sort of thing. The singer was only a talent to be shaped entirely by us. But the Beatles, you see, had ideas about what they wanted to do, and at that time they lacked the knowledge of techniques to bring it off. At an early session we had a bit of a howl because I suggested playing up the bass guitar. The boys felt very huffy because their sound was being altered. But you must understand that in those days this whole notion of rock performers as free souls was simply unheard of. I didn't like their songs, and I was searching for a hit for them. Finally, I thought I had found one: 'How Do You Do It?' by Mitch Murray.

"They actually recorded the song, but they didn't like it very much. And they didn't do it very well. Somewhere as a matter of fact, we still have that recording. But it was never released. They came to me after the session and said: 'We just don't think that song is right for us.' But I told them straight out that I still thought it was a potential hit and a hit was what they needed. But they still wanted to do one of their own songs. They felt that they could write a better song. So I said, 'Go ahead, but remember that you're turning down a hit.' And they did it; they came up with 'Please Please Me,' and I was delighted with it. And I told them that they had a sure number-one tune. I gave 'How Do You Do It' to Jerry and the Pacemakers later on, and they recorded it successfully."

"I have always assumed that in the early days the Beatles worked entirely without studio musicians," I said.

"Yes, until we recorded the song 'Yesterday' and with the exception of the Andy White incident, they always played all their own music—which was also something very new in the record industry. I filled in on the piano now and again, but that was just to help out."

"Did you ever find their inability to read or write music a handicap?"

"Not really, no. In the early days, when they had a new song, they stood around me with their guitars while I sat on a high stool, and they simply sang the song to me. In this way, I would get to know it pretty well. Then I would suggest some things in the arrangement: what to do for the beginning, the middle, and the ending, the solos, you know, and I would always try to demonstrate what I meant at the piano. However, in the very early days they had trouble transcribing the piano sound to their own instruments. Being guitar players, they always thought of finger shapes on the guitar and not piano-chord figures. Seeing my fingers on the piano keys confused them. So I started to learn the guitar to try to match up with them. In the meantime, Paul bought an old upright piano and he started playing the piano and overtook me because I can't play guitar at all well, while he plays piano very well indeed. But even before that they would whistle a musical idea or finger it on the guitar. Because, after all, music doesn't really have to be written down to be music."

"Perhaps," I suggested to George Martin, "the very ability to write music might limit one's musical thinking, since you would tend to think only in terms of a kind of music which exists as written notes, if you see what I mean."

"I think that's very possible in the case of the Beatles. From the beginning they were primitive and were free to seek their own solutions to problems. It is true that a musical education might have shortened that search, but it also might have made them end up with something far less original than they have created in their own way."

"When did you start using additional musicians with the Beatles?"

"With the song 'Yesterday.' It was really Paul's pigeon. It was more him than anybody else. He wrote 'Yesterday' and none of us were sure what to do with it. In fact, I said, 'I can't imagine Ringo bashing away on an upbeat on this song.' So finally I said, 'Look, Paul, the only thing to do is for you to go down into the studio with your guitar and record the song, and then we'll listen to it and decide what to put on top of it.' And we did just that. We listened to it many times, and I said as diplomatically as I could, 'Honestly, Paul, the only thing I can think of doing is to put strings on it.' That didn't go down very well, as you can imagine. And I said it with great trepidation because I knew what they thought of strings. And Paul said, 'Well, we don't want any of those Mantovani strings, you know.' And he wanted to know if we couldn't do something smaller than that, you know—just use a few strings. So I said, 'What about a string quartet?' which was sort of going back to my work producing classical Baroque music. And Paul said, 'That sounds like a good idea.' So he came to my flat one evening and I went through the tape with him. I was getting his musical ideas—how he saw the thing in terms of a string quartet. I started taking notes—acting like a tape recorder as it were—and eventually I actually wrote an arrangement with his ideas in mind."

"This is probably a sticky point," I said with some hesitation, knowing how cautiously George Martin guarded against making the impression that the great recordings of the Beatles were his conceptions, "but I think it's the major musical intrigue in your relationship with the Beatles. Was Paul actually whistling the various voicings of a string quartet? Was he indicating specifically what the cello would play and what the viola would play? In other words, to what extent was Paul aware, for instance, of what a string quartet is capable of doing?"

"Well, my goodness, after all he was very aware. You make him sound a bit of an idiot. He was no fool. And he knew darn well that a cello was a deep voice and that a violin was a high one. Obviously he wasn't aware of the range of each instrument or the way it performed—which is something you learn in music school. But he would offer a musical idea for a phrase here and there. This was typical of our collaboration. It was no more or less than any musical phrase I might offer to them in the course of another arrangement we were working on. The Beatles, I can say safely, are responsible for everything we hear in their music. I would never pretend to be the musical ghost behind the Beatles. On the other hand, it was a matter of collaboration. But it's difficult to describe for you exactly how that collaboration worked. If you want to get down to asking, 'Well, now, that note—did it come from Paul or John?' it becomes awfully petty, and Paul, I'm sure, would be upset if I indicated that this note was mine and so forth. But it is safe to say that the music came from the boys themselves. When I first met them, they were really very illiterate, musically. With success, however, they changed very greatly. They started becoming increasingly aware of things which they had not previously found in music. 'Yesterday' came about basically because a song required something more than their normal musical accompaniment. In fact, the one thing that 'Yesterday' suggested to the boys was that the instruments which they were able to play were not adequate for their musical ideas, which were evolving. Prior to that, it had been something like inverted pride which had made them refuse studio musicians. They wanted to make all of the music themselves. But once they became aware of tone color and what other instruments could lend to their music, they began to think about involving other musicians. In fact, it was at that stage that they became interested in electronic music."

"What was their first use of electronically produced sound? Was it 'Strawberry Fields'?"

"Oh, no, it was long before that. Let's see—on 'Revolver' there was a track called—hmmm, oh dear, something—well, it's the last track . . . yes, that's right, 'Tomorrow Never Knows.' Anyway, on that track they did something special. They had all gotten themselves little tape recorders, and they used to enjoy making loops, you know, a short piece of tape with a recorded fragment on it which is glued end-on-end into a continuous band that plays over and over again. They brought in various loops in envelopes, and they wanted to know if we could use them. This wasn't synthesized sound, because the boys had no access to that kind of equipment. But what they did on these loops could hardly be defined as real music, though some of it was made from guitars and piano. A lot of it was just vocal sounds, like laughter overdubbed many times and speeded up. In fact, the track I mentioned, 'Tomorrow Never Knows,' contains a kind of seagull noise which is actually laughter speeded up.

"The Beatles were just beginning to become aware of musical experimentation. In fact, using these techniques in 'Tomorrow Never Knows' was a result of their listening to records. They are very enthusiastic collectors. If one of them found a new sound he went to the others and said, 'It's the greatest!' Probably that's how they happened to hear a recording of something by Stockhausen, and they wanted to do something like it.

"The Beatles and I all changed a great deal over the years we worked together. In recording 'I Want to Hold Your Hand' I was trying to capture on tape the sound the boys made in a live performance, or slightly better than that. I made suggestions to tidy things up. And also, I was very much the boss and they were the pupils. They were virtually under my thumb," Martin laughed. "This naturally changed with their success and power. Today they are considerably wealthier than I am. Naturally they wanted more to say about what goes on. At that time, all over the world, youth was realizing its power—both in wealth and in numbers—and it wanted to have more to say about its fate. So consequently, with something like 'Strawberry Fields,' which John wrote, he had some nebulous ideas in the back of his mind, and my role at that point was to get that nebulous idea into concrete form. So I had to get out of his mind what kind of sounds he was thinking about and how he wanted to express himself, and try to translate all of that into real fact—into music, you see. I think "Strawberry Fields' was one of the best things the Beatles ever did. Curiously enough, it wasn't the A side—the major side—of the single. 'Penny Lane' was the A side. I argued long and hard with the boys to make 'Strawberry Fields' the A side as opposed to 'Penny Lane,' but I lost. Paul had written 'Penny Lane' and John wrote 'Strawberry Fields.' Paul was worried about the commercial potential of John's song. He felt his own tune, 'Penny Lane,' was more commercial. Brian Epstein backed Paul. I lost."

"The Beatles surely brought about a phenomenal change in the popular-music industry," I said.

"Yes, I think there is no question that the Beatles have improved the whole pop music field in innumerable ways. I was delighted to be part of it as their—let us say—'realizer.' They certainly suggested the potential power available to talented young people."

IT'S A BIRD, IT'S A PLANE, IT'S TOM JONES

It was the winter of 1968, and somewhere in the weary world people were groveling through slush to get to dull jobs in dismal offices. But on the roof of the Continental Hyatt House on the Sunset Strip in Los Angeles, we were lazing in the opulent rays of the late-afternoon sun while spotless waiters delivered sumptuous sandwiches and iced tea to umbrellad tables at poolside.

The phone sounds and a guest answers it. "Is there a Mr. Tom Jones here?" he calls out politely.

"Sorry," a British youth with long, stringy hair and red-tipped pimples says, "he's not here just now." But most of the members of

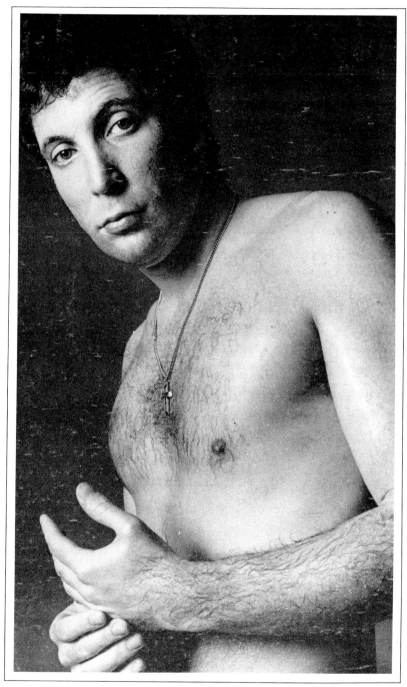

Tom Jones

Tom's distinguished band are present, checking their watches now and again so they aren't late for the day's television taping.

Meanwhile a large, pink musician is dripping on me. "Tom's a delight," he says between tireless laps around the pool. "Nicest chap in the business. And, of course, a major talent!"

I nod reluctantly and pretend to be deeply absorbed in a magazine. But the musician keeps dripping on me. "Tom's got the best voice going. A really *major* talent!" he insists.

With these words of esteem for his boss, the wet pianist plunges back into the pool.

In the midst of this Hyatt paradise, a tall, dark stranger ambles into view. Whispers rise rapidly as he strolls across the artificial grass carpet and among the plastic shrubs and palms. The musicians, upon seeing this imposing figure, snap to preposterous attention. "Hi, Tom!"

The two dozen women who are freely giving themselves to the sun stir conspicuously. Everyone's attention is on the doorway where the tall, dark stranger is talking to a manager-looking man.

My God, could it really be he?

Yes, indeed, folks: presenting the Greatest Voice in the World, starring Tom Jones and His Entire Body!

The next time I was confronted by the phenomenon of Mr. Jones was later that same year in the overflowing arena of Madison Square Garden in New York, where the Great Man Himself was scheduled to display his exceptional endowments in exchange for a mere king's ransom.

The air of expectancy was so intense at the Garden that I felt certain we had assembled to hear the premiere of the Sermon on the Mount. It was like getting lost in the ladies' room. There they were under their teased, tormented, and tinted hairdos, the Amazons of America's suburbia with their cameras and their purses clutched to their breasts.

There they are in the big arena to see Mr. Tom Jones do it all for real! Do it even more than he dares to do it on television!

The mammoth matriarchs of the western world are there with their fledgling daughters, junior tinted, teased, and sprayed. The clothes are right off the rack, not a wrinkle or mark of humanity.

Also present at the Garden are some husbands—one-button fellas with razor cuts who carry little cardboard trays of cola and hot dogs. Hubbies who buy the five-dollar picture program, who smile nicely as the little lady gores ol' Tom with her eyes, content to watch while the wife gets turned on by Tom, gets sex without penetration.

I remember sitting in a pathetically plastic flat in London in 1967, listening to Jones tell me all about it. "I simply love the ladies," he said. "I love them . . . all the moms and all the little curly tops too. And I really want to make them happy. You know," he intoned in his hopelessly fake upper-class British accent, "I really love to get up there and make them *all* happy."

These recollections of my first encounter with Tom Jones are interrupted by a swell of sound and a sweep of energy at Madison Square Garden. It is as if a miracle is about to take place. The sound gradually rises, with intermittent, hysterically pitched screams filtering through the mayhem. Slowly the groan becomes a long, shrill cry of bliss. And, BOOM! There he is! *It's a bird! It's a plane! It's Tom Jones!* He comes on like a boxer, already in a sweat, doing it—dancing, prancing, shadow boxing with his hips and shaking his head. Bump, bump, bump. There go the cameras, like three thousand strobe lights flashing all around me.

Now I can't see a thing. The ladies are on their feet. A wave of enthralled outcries mixes with the screaming: "Do it, Tommy!" "Come on, sweetheart, let's see it all!" "Do it again! Do it again, Tommy! Do it for your mama!"

He's wearing a tuxedo that fits like formal, black skin. There are lots of major comments all around me about Tommy's pants. But some of the women also talk about his face. He's got the kind of face you'd expect to find in a coal mine in Wales: pockmarked, old Chippendale topped with a blackish tassel. He's what many call resistably attractive, but the ladies at Madison Square Garden are eating him alive. Of course, they don't listen to much of his singing. And there's little applause for the songs. The outcry is mainly in response to his bumps and grinds. Tommy's a pretty good dancer. But, goodness, he sure sweats a lot. Everywhere you look, the women are throwing him handkerchiefs, hoping he'll toss one back soaked with some souvenir perspiration.

Meanwhile he's singing "Fly Me to the Moon" in the manner of Frank Sinatra and "Try a Little Tenderness" in the style of Tony Bennett. He's got a good, strong voice and operates with it somewhere in the suburbs of showmanship. He begins by letting the good ladies know he's up there for them: "Good evening ladies . . . and gentlemen," he exclaims. "Some people can't stop drinking. Some people can't stop smoking. But me . . . !" There is a drum roll suggesting something incredibly lewd, and then, as the girls giggle and sigh with shocked relief (and disappointment), he sings "I Can't Stop Loving You" in the fashion of Otis Redding.

Now Jones titillates the ladies by talking about his orchestrator: "He arranges everything for me . . . well, not *everything!*" Screams of laughter. And, mind you, he does all of this with a large crucifix dangling from a heavy silver ID bracelet.

Ten minutes into the act Jones loosens his bow tie. Fifteen minutes later his jacket comes off. Ten minutes after that he slips out of his velvet vest. Delirium sets in among the spectators. He undoes the top four buttons of his shirt. Drum roll and rim shot! And then he sings "Satisfaction" in the style of Mick Jagger.

What is all this fuss about Tom Jones? In the era that was renowned for its highly inventive popular music, how could the massive audience that disdained rock 'n' roll as vulgar adore such an obviously vulgar performer? It seems to me that Tom Jones is a minuscule example of how sensibilities have been compromised by television. His entire stage show is really nothing more or less than uncensored "live television." He was the electronic lover of many bored housewives of the sixties and seventies, who equally scorned rock freaks and feminists. Tom Jones was the ultimate dildo: a 23-inch color-TV pinup of a man! And a damn good male impersonator!

ODYSSEUS IN JEANS:
KRIS KRISTOFFERSON

Slow fade-in. Los Angeles. A hustler and a woman come into focus. They hunch against a cigarette machine near the entrance of the Troubadour, a seedy hangout on Santa Monica Boulevard. The man is attractively derelict, wearing hustler's rumpled midnight-cowboy gear. The woman is perfectly tubular, except for evidence of a seven-month pregnancy. She wears a Moroccan sheath fastened with a row of seventy tiny buttons running from her breast, across the ominous abundance of her belly, down to her fragile ankles and large feet. A cloud of frazzled hair surrounds her emaciated white face, from which two large almond-shaped eyes peer out at the world. Her nar-

Kris Kristofferson

row mouth is fixed in an expression of indifference as she slowly clamps her long, thin fingers around the hustler's belt buckle and pulls him into the steaming crush of the bar. The man, totally stoned, follows like a dreamer . . . until the director yells, "CUT!"

The man is Kris Kristofferson. He's not a hustler but a movie star, a friend, and a singer-songwriter whose abrupt rise to fame in the early seventies resulted in his starring in the film *Cisco Pike* with co-stars Viva and Karen Black. It is Viva with whom he has just completed the sixteenth attempt to capture an entrance on film.

Kris and I became friends just before his first album for Columbia Records was released. I was working on a CBS television project in the early 1970s with producer Roger Gimble. A friend of mine, who produced country music in Nashville, told me about a remarkable new talent, giving me a mug shot of a handsomely roughcut guy and a demotape of a couple of his tunes. Eventually Kris and I met, and I introduced him to Gimble, saying: "We ought to use this guy. He's going to be a star."

A year later I went out to Los Angeles to interview him.

"Jeez," Kris tells me in his exquisite Texas drawl while he and Viva sit over dinner at the Aware Inn on Sunset Boulevard, "we spent all day filming some puny scene like that entrance at the Troubadour, and then we have to get right to it and finish off a really good scene where we get to do some acting in less than half an hour. Lord, it's worse than the pressure of a recording session!"

Kris is not your average inarticulate and job-hungry actor, and it will not be too many more years before directors learn that he likes to have a good deal to say about the quality and tone of his performances in films.

When he gets up from the table to make a phone call, I ask Viva, "What do you think of Kris?"

"Fab-U-lous," she intones in the very flat voice I have learned to expect of her from her roles in Andy Warhol's movies.

"And what do you think of him as an actor?"

She flashes a mannequinlike grimace and arches her long neck. "Fab-U-lous," she says again.

Kristofferson ambles back to the table, lights up a Bull Durham cigarette from his fourth pack of the day, and slouches in his chair.

"That guy is a real wimp," he complains of the businessman he has just been talking to on the phone. "He's the type of cat who keeps telling you how much more he knows about music than you do and all about his thirty-five years of experience. You know the kind I mean? I finally got good and fed up and told him, 'Man, you ain't got no thirty-five years of experience behind you. What you got is one year of experience thirty-five times!'"

Though a newcomer to the entertainment industry at the time, Kristofferson could get away with speaking his mind because he was the hottest thing going in Nashville. At the annual Country Music Association awards show he walked off with the song-of-the-year award for his "Sunday Mornin' Comin' Down," and he had just been named songwriter of the year by the Nashville Songwriters' Association. The success of Kris Kristofferson annoyed some of the conservative folks on Nashville's famous Music Row. To them he was a hippie weirdo, a long-haired outsider with a college education and wearing suede bell-bottoms, climbing right up there onto the stage of the venerable Grand Ole Opry to accept the highest award in the field of country music.

"Anyway, my music isn't exactly country," Kris is saying as we drive toward the hotel where he can clean up after a long day in front of the cameras. "I think it started down in Brownsville, Texas. Of course, I've been influenced by a lot of things since I was a kid, but what got deepest down into my gut was that border Mexican music—basically simple melodies where the emotion in the song is up front . . . Mexican harmonies . . . simple two-part things . . . with lots of feeling," he explains. "By the time I was in high school—in the midfifties—I was out in California. Of course, I knew who all the country singers were, but Hank Williams was my big hero then, and he was pretty unknown out on the Coast, except for country fans. And there weren't many country fans in those days. But what I dug about country music (and still do about the really good tunes) is that they're honest expressions of emotion."

We swing into his motel and go up to his room. Kristofferson wearily collapses onto the bed, where his twelve-string guitar rests like a lover on the pillow. Kris hunches down over his memories and his guitar, squeezing his soft blue eyes closed, as his voice—battered by booze and Bull Durham into a raspy baritone—talks and sings lyrics that already seem to be yellowed with age.

" 'Casey's Last Ride' started out as nothing more than a line and an idea, an image of subways in London. 'Casey joins the hollow sounds/of silent people walking down/the stairway to the subway/and the shadows down below.' You know, something like that. And then it just laid in my head. I didn't finish it, but I was always thinking about those lines until one night when I was driving from New Orleans to Morgan City, where I was gonna go out in the Gulf on one of those offshore oil rigs. And tired? Like three a.m. in a bad rainstorm and I had three flat tires. It's not the time to be writing songs. And that damned song came to me. All of it—even with that middle section that I really like: 'Oh, she said, Casey, it's been so long since I've seen you./Here, she said, just a kiss to make a body smile./See, she said, I've put on new stockings just to please you./Lord, she said, Casey, can you only stay a while?' It came out of nowhere. When you're writing you're just holdin' up the pen."

Kristofferson often admitted that his songs are autobiographical, a natural enough thing for a troubadour. "The tune I wrote that first hit people hard was 'Jody and the Kid.' I wrote it back when I was splitting up with my old lady, and I was taking my little girl around to places I worked at—like the Tally Ho Tavern, where I used to tend bar. It's a kind of a publike old place over on Sixteenth Avenue South in Nashville and it's really funky. Some old guy, one of the regulars, saw the little girl and me comin' in. And he said, 'Hey, looka younder. There comes critter and the kid.' Well, I didn't think 'Flash!'—there's a song! But it kinda stuck in my head, I guess, 'cause it was a real sad time for me. I hated losing the kids, especially the little girl, 'cause she's my faithful fan. Later, when I went down to work on the Gulf, I finished the song.

"To me," Kris drawls quietly as he strips off his black turtleneck, "the purpose of any kind of writing or any kind of art form is to move people—to laughter or to crying or to anger or to something. But you've gotta move them . . . emotionally and not intellectually."

I look at him as he speaks. Kris was starting to show signs of a narrow spare tire in those days—a trophy, no doubt, of countless nights on the town with his drinking buddies. As film stardom gradually overtook him, he finally kept his often-stated promise to shape up. "Hardest damn thing I ever did!" he told me years later. Even back in 1971, I notice while he talks that his handsome face is showing the unmistakable puffiness of a drinker. "Maybe I'm into booze," he confesses to me. "Grass is just fine, but booze and me are old friends." He smiles as he orders two vodkas and ginger ale from room service and then disappears into the bathroom, from which he shouts over the sound of the shower. "Don't get me wrong. I'm not a political man, but I'm also not a bigot. When I wrote 'Blame It on the Stones,' I was mad 'cause Jagger was given an inordinate sentence just for having something like two pep pills and one joint in his pocket. I identified with the Rolling Stones because the people in my own family were always putting down musicians as drug addicts and the like. Yet people that I saw in every walk of life—you know, doctors, lawyers, students, members of bridge clubs—they were on some kind of escape trip, too, whether it was booze, uppers, downers, or grass. And so why nail Jagger? I hate indignation."

Kris is the son of an ex-military man (later an air-operations manager for Aramco) who died shortly after this interview. From Brownsville, Texas, where he was born, Kris moved with his family to California, where he later attended Pomona College. "I wasn't a rebel when I was eight, but I was a rebel when I was living in California. Maybe that's just because I was a different age. But I think I went back more to what I really liked—for instance, country music. But when I was in California I was always embarrassed to say I liked country songs, and I'd roll the windows up in my car and listen to Hank Williams. I was a creative writing major in my undergraduate years, and I was getting some good stuff written." As a matter of fact, he won four out of twenty prizes in the *Atlantic*'s collegiate short-story contest and was subsequently awarded a Rhodes scholarship to Oxford University.

"When I got to England," he tells me as he climbs into a black suede and leather outfit, "I really got involved in literature. I was excited about William Blake and Shakespeare and John Donne. My old man, he was in the Army, so he thought I was doing just fine, but I really wasn't sure why I was at Oxford. I can remember consciously compromising myself and saying that I was going to play according to the rules and if some idiot was up in front of the class saying something stupid and he was on some kind of an ego trip, I was not going to cut him down or anything. I was going to agree with him and I was gonna study, and I was going to give him back exactly what he wanted, regardless of whether it was right or not. And I did it. But I really didn't like schoolwork. And I never wanted to be a schoolteacher. Every day at Oxford, they kept correcting my accent and my grammar and kept tellin' me I sounded like a hick, and I kept right on talking my own way. But that's not much resistance to authority by comparison to the way students stood up for their ideals in the sixties, but back when I was in school things were different; most of us were just damned glad to be in college, and we kept our mouths shut. What I was doing at Oxford was what somebody else wanted me to do. And it took a complete tearing loose to get free of it and of my family. I had to drop straight to the bottom. But that took a lot more years. So anyway, when I left Oxford, I got married and went into the Army. I was an officer when I went in and went through jump school and on to flight school. When I got out I was a captain. And I was on the way to teaching English lit. up at West Point, which was, as far as the family was concerned, a nice place to be. And I know I didn't want any part of it, and I was just foolin' myself into thinking I might dig it 'cause I went up there and visited the place, and it was graduation time and it was beautiful and there were all those pretty girls out seein' their beaux, and I went around with a major who showed me the stuff and he started talkin' about lesson plans and gave me these books that I had to read ahead of time, and this vague feelin' of despair began creeping over my body, and I remember I rode back on the bus . . . I still didn't know that I wasn't gonna do it . . . didn't know till I got to Nashville and all of a sudden I saw real people! They were crazy! They were alive and they were creatin' things . . . writing songs! They were all up where I hadn't been for years, 'cause I mean you're really *dead* when you're in the Army.

"Well, it was the roughest thing I'd ever done in my life. I just turned my back on the whole thing: education, respectability, family, past, and position. For a year and a half I worked at Columbia Records Studios in Nashville, cleaning ashtrays and doing things like that. I got offers to work for music publishing companies, but I knew I would never do the writing I wanted to do if I got involved in a job with responsibilities. Then I got a job bartending at the Tally Ho. My old lady wanted the good life, so right about the time that she and I were about to split up, well, she got pregnant. I knew I was going to need more money than the sixty bucks a week I was makin', so I went down to the Gulf to fly the helicopters on the off-shore oil rigs, and I did that for about twenty months.

"I didn't quit that job until just a year ago. I really panicked, because I had five hundred a month in child support to pay, and I had the remainder of a ten-thousand-dollar hospital bill that I was payin' on 'cause my little boy had to have an operation. And I thought, 'Oh God, I'm gonna be thrown in jail.' And I came back to Nashville. They were doing the Johnny Cash Show on television and a friend of mine, named Mickey Newberry, was stayin' in the hotel where they were runnin' the Cash show. He had a chance to meet all these people that we never had a chance to pitch songs to before. So we were gettin' to meet big people in the music industry. Just like that, a publisher agreed to pay me enough money to meet my commitment until the show was over, as long as I was pitchin' songs and I was gettin' stuff recorded. Out of that I met Roger Miller, and he cut three of my songs. 'Bobby McGee' was the first song of mine he recorded. And then Fred Foster of Monument Records in Nashville came up during the session when Roger was cuttin' the third song, and he said straight out: 'I understand you're having some financial problems.' And I said, 'Well, a little bit.' You know, he bailed me out of the whole mess. Gave me a loan that paid off the hospital bill, kept me solvent, and then I got a job working out here on a TV special for John Hartford with Mickey Newberry that gave me some more money, and I haven't had to work a lick since!"

Work, to Kristofferson, was something other than writing songs. As he sees it, if he could make money writing tunes, then he didn't have to work. Within a few months of the release of the film *Cisco Pike*, Kristofferson songs were the most sought-after tunes in the music world. At that time, there had already been fifty different recorded versions of "Me and Bobby McGee" alone.

"Cheers!" he exclaims with a great smile as he downs the last of the vodka. "Want to hear a new one I'm just finishing?" He pulls his twelve-string comfortably into his lap and picks out a song: "Around the honky tonks/searchin' for a sign/gettin' by on gettin' high/on women, words, and wine."

Kris and I walk out into the warm Los Angeles night. We get into his car and drive through Laurel Canyon to the San Fernando Valley where Kris had promised to meet an old girlfriend. Sailing over the dark hills and peering down at the vast sea of lights stretching limitlessly across the valley floor, I realize that the place I'm looking at has been totally transformed since I had grown up there, when it was nothing but unbroken acres of grass and groves.

Finally, we roll up to the posh and very conservative restaurant called Tail of the Cock on Ventura Boulevard, where the attendant gives both Kris and me an incredulous look and reluctantly drives off to park our car. We head into the bar. "How about this film you're doing now?" I ask him as we look around for Kris's date.

"Well," he laughs, "I lucked into that one, too. The guy who cast *Five Easy Pieces* had seen me when I did my first appearance at the Troubadour with Linda Ronstadt, and he liked me. I got to know him out at Jack Nicholson's house. You see, I had come to L.A. 'cause Janis Joplin died, and I was pretty broken up about it. I didn't want to go to her funeral or anything, I just wanted to know if anybody knew what had actually happened.

"Well, anyway, I was in Los Angeles, so they asked me to read for the part in *Cisco Pike*. Next day, they made a screen test of me to see if I could act, and then I split for Nashville. About a day or so later, they called and said I got the part, so I came back out to California. A young director named Bill Norton wrote the script. Karen Black plays my old lady, and Viva plays this wealthy chick who picks me up. I play a cat who used to be a musician but who got into dealing drugs to make a living."

After searching the bar, we finally find Kris's date waiting for us at a table in the restaurant. She's gorgeous. He says, "I'm just lucky with the ladies. I get really lonely being on the road all the time."

"He's a poetic truck driver," one illustrious lady of song once confided to me. "He has had most of us, and he's had most of us more than once. There's the great lady of song who made him park his car a block down the street when he stayed overnight with her. Mature, sophisticated women who usually scoff at rock stars look at Kris as if he were the ultimate male. His sincerity is his best weapon."

By now it is very late. We walk Kris's date to her car and Kris says good night. We drive back to his hotel. I ask him, "Do you ever feel that you're standing between two worlds?"

As he drops me at the curb, he replies a bit sadly. "I've felt that way all my damned life. I really have the feeling that I'm a perpetual outsider. Every place I go it's the same. I've never been part of any group or any party or hung around with any one friend or anything like that. The women I know today won't be the ones I'll know tomorrow. I'm friends with a lot of people but not anybody's best friend. I got to keep moving and living if I'm gonna keep on writing. You see, to tell you the truth, I'm a scared writer. I never know if I'm gonna be able to write another song."

GOOD-BYE
JANIS JOPLIN

On October 4, 1970, I was in New York, and Janis Joplin was in Los Angeles. She didn't show up at Sunset Sound Studios, where she was recording a new album called *Pearl*. Paul Rothchild, her producer, gave in to a strange premonition and sent someone over to the Landmark Motor Hotel to see why the twenty-seven-year-old singer wasn't answering her phone. She didn't respond to repeated efforts to awaken her by banging on the door, so the desk clerk used a passkey. Janis was lying wedged between the bed and a nightstand, wearing a short nightgown. Her lips were bloody when they turned

Janis Joplin

her over, and her nose was broken. She clutched four dollars and fifty cents in her hand.

An hour later my phone rang in New York and one of her friends told me that Joplin was dead. I hung up without saying anything. I didn't want to think about it, but all night I kept seeing a girl sitting in frumpy disarray in the back row of a little theater on Washington Street in San Francisco in 1966, her legs thrown over the back of the seat in front of her, chewing gum and incessantly bouncing her head to the beat of the sound that Big Brother and the Holding Company were pouring into the empty auditorium. Her name was Janis and she had just come up from Texas with Chet Helm, who was managing Big Brother and who was trying, with a commune called the Family Dog, to do some new things in the world of the San Francisco counterculture.

The music stopped while everyone took a break. "Hey," Peter Albin, leader of Big Brother, announced, fetching the little ugly girl and pulling her down the aisle toward the stage, "this here is ol' Janis—best damn singer in the world!" She looked kind of haggard for her age and she had that bittersweet, heart-of-gold tough nonchalance of a beat-up old broad. There was nothing fancy about Janis. Shy and therefore apt to express herself in sudden bursts of liberated embarrassment, she always felt best standing off by herself or hidden within the warm folds of a rock group. That day, only five years before her death, she was just joining Big Brother and the Holding Company, a favorite local blues band that was then collaborating with me in a show called *Blast!*

A couple of months later, when Helm opened the Avalon Ballroom, Janis and Big Brother became the unofficial house band. Almost every weekend night you could climb the stairs on Sutter Street and wander around the blimp hangar of a dance hall and find Janis sitting over a Coke upstairs in the snack bar or leaning against a wall near the bandstand listening to the music. A few of the kids recognized her and said a casual "Hi," but mostly she stood by herself, straightening her rings or her antique cape like a middle-aged wallflower at a Southern VFW Saturday night hop.

Men rarely made any big plays for Janis in those days, and even in the unpretentious society of hippies she was considered an introvert.

But once in front of an audience something fantastic would happen to Janis Joplin. She was the lioness of rock, performing dances that bore the most sensational resemblance to the Kabuki dance of the lions, in which men in very long and colorful manes toss their heads in controlled frenzy. And she moved like a deranged dancer, while belting out a shattering emotional sound ... cross-stepping from one side of the stage to the other, making an urgent sort of pleading gesture toward the audience with her outstretched hands. An agony of expression; perspired and disheveled and furious and real. Then when she stationed herself at a microphone and voiced a kind of stuttering, staggering outcry that she had learned from Otis Redding—a singer she greatly admired—the audience went to its feet and Janis beat an angular rhythm with one foot that punctuated and articulated her gigantic outpouring. As a performer, she was everything that the white American music world had long abhorred: excessive, physical, almost out of control. There was utterly no Doris Day in Janis. She was so intense as a performer that even the traditionalism of her lyrics about love, sex, and loss was overwhelmed by the sheer magnitude of her singing.

When I interviewed Janis in January of 1968, she had the Monterey pop festival behind her, so she was beginning to understand her own power, although she was still relatively unknown. "I got a good voice," she grunted, wiping her mouth with the back of her hand and then removing her famous fur hat. "What I mean is that the pipes in my throat from here to here are made real good." And she smiled self-consciously. "I'm learning to sing," she said. "I mean I've only been singing about a year now and so I've got a lot to learn. But I figure that maybe in about another three years I'm going to be a real good singer."

Three years later Janis Joplin was dead. But she had kept her promise. She had become a great singer. She successfully revived an old cliché for a new generation. She was the ultimate embodiment of our sense of tragedy: a concept by which to measure pain. We chose her as the quintessential loser, and she perfectly and willingly lived up to the role. She never disappointed her audience, neither in the tragic nature of her death nor in the ironic perfection of her last album, *Pearl,* the name by which some of her intimates knew her.

But for me the name has a different significance. Constant irritation produces pearls; a pearl is a disease of the oyster. Gustave Flaubert said that the artist is a disease of society. Janis was a disease of America's gigantic alienation. She was a pearl.

Kris Kristofferson tells a story about Janis. She confessed something to him that she must have told to several of her friends, for she made the same tragic remark to me in San Francisco when I last saw her.

Kristofferson recalls that Janis was performing in Los Angeles and asked him to have a drink with her at a seedy bar across the tracks from the groupie-infested Tropicana Motel on Santa Monica Boulevard, where many rock stars stayed. Kris spent a couple of hours with her after her sold-out, smash performance. Then he walked her across the tracks to the shabby room where she collapsed onto her rumpled bed. Kris remembers being concerned by her massive fatigue. "Are you all right?" he asked. Janis half opened her eyes and smiled bitterly. "Sure," she muttered, "I'm just working on a new tune in my head," she mumbled in her rusty voice. "I'm gonna call it something like this: 'I Just Made Love to Twenty-five Thousand People, But I'm Goin' Home Alone.'"

Then she went to sleep.

THE DREAM IS OVER

When Ken Kesey and Paul Krassner asked me to write the lead article for *The Last Supplement of the Whole Earth Catalogue* (which they jointly edited), I had grown deeply disappointed with the world of rock. I felt that the ideals of the youth movement that had been so attractive to me had utterly collapsed and that my friends had vanished. Haight-Ashbury and the East Village were battle zones where idealistic young people were hustled, beaten, robbed, or—like a naive kid named Groovy—brutally murdered by freeloaders, pimps, and drug dealers. The rock festivals that had started out so euphorically at Monterey were now high-exploitation events where greed and violence shattered the idyllic mood. At Altamont bikers hired for crowd control battered the public with pool cues and stabbed one spectator. Meanwhile, the record business had become a huge industry in which rock stars—who were often senselessly cheated by their own managers—gradually became self-centered and outrageous brats who exploited women, squandered huge sums of money on nonsense, and lived lives that totally contradicted the idealistic lyrics of their top-ten and gold-record tunes. The youth movement's celebration of freedom and intuition and spirituality had degenerated into ignorance, irrationality, and pointless anti-intellectualism.

Things had drastically changed. Many people no longer thought every infantile prank was a profound social gesture. Our world of "good vibes" was becoming dangerous. Our friends were perishing from overdoses. The optimistic slogans of 1967 had been replaced by barbarous rantings. And as we looked on with dismay, we saw a staggeringly self-centered element rise out of the youth movement. The most clever of these people created a hierarchy—a hip establishment—that used every ploy of the straight culture they claimed to disdain. The hip establishment dominated underground publications, political organizations, and record companies and occupied other positions of power, manipulating the vast youth network to their own ends and for their own profit. Meanwhile, the sickest of the urban terrorists politicized their psychoses, emerging as fanatic bombers and destroyers—indulging in their paranoid psychodramas on the streets, where anyone could become their victim. Not until years later, in a film called *Taxi Driver,* did many come to recognize how many maniacs had been celebrated as heroes.

There were many such psychopaths, but Charles Manson was the ultimate hippie madman. Astonishingly, for a brief moment he was even embraced by some members of the Weather Underground as a soldier in the cause of liberation. Then the horrendous truth about Manson became apparent to even the most militant, and all recoiled and wanted no part of him. But Charles Manson didn't simply *happen.* He was created by a time and a place and by a people who believed that all "truth" would be miraculously and automatically revealed to them either through violence against "the system" or through drug-induced revelations—or a combination of both. These believers in revelation started out with the ideal of reexamining the dominance of Western morality and politics and ended with such an extremist contempt for traditional learning that they totally lacked a sense of history. And so, methodically and ignorantly and tragically, they restaged the French Revolution, bringing down with equal passion all that was right and all that was wrong with our world. We have not recovered yet.

The decline I witnessed of a world of free spirits and idealists was so depressing that I wrote an essay that many of my peers—including Krassner—thought unduly pessimistic. I wrote the article "The Dream Is Over" in March 1971. More than a decade later, as I look back on what I wrote, I am more convinced than ever that it was a valid picture of the times. As John Lennon said: "We blew it."

Charles Manson announced the new decade: "Death is psychosomatic," he said. "I am just a mirror. If God is One, what is bad?" he asked. His message was terrifying and inscrutable. It promised the marriage of two outlaw cultures: the hood and the head, making room for the complex metaphysical gangster saga of our era, decreeing the ruthless realism and the grisly cinema verité of the Altamont rock festival. It also resounded of the romantic vision of death which haunted Poe and Swinburne and the whole romantic movement:

> But the decadence of history is looking for a pawn
> To a nightmare of knowledge he opens up the gate
> A blinding revelation is served upon his plate
> That beneath the greatest love is a hurricane of hate.
> —from "Crucifixion," by Phil Ochs

And so death walked into our world, where we thought no one would ever die. Like the fragile princess who was destined to prick her finger on the needle of a spinning wheel and fall into eternal sleep, we had been marked for death almost from the beginning. A strange and great impending shadow fell over the profile of a whole generation.

But death had always been part of our mystique. After all, weren't both Dylan and McCartney "wished dead"? It was not too long ago that we reveled in rumors that they had died and been shrewdly re-placed by doubles. And wasn't it an awareness of war and annihila-tion that was the prime motive for our nervous sensualism? And hadn't every summer ended with the Red Specter himself walking into our rooms and changing his face fourteen times before taking away one or two of our most precious idols? Ceremonies such as the 1968 "funeral process" down Haight Street had been an integral part of the theatrical rites of the children of the Bomb. One earthquake does more in sixty seconds to shake our belief in the stability of our world than two centuries of philosophical reflection. Our celebration of life hadn't fooled anyone. We grew up with the fear of extinction.

Now we are realistic enough to recognize that the evolution of our alternative life-style into high fashion and show biz is a burial in plastic, a sort of living death if not exactly a matter of death itself. Contrasting with our recognition of the inevitable demise of our pure and impossible belief in the inherent goodness of humanity were celebrations of optimism and sensuality that were so hysterical that they almost succeeded in obscuring the fear and pessimism that is at the core of our generation. Monterey and Woodstock, the Be-ins and Love-ins and the private festivities in living rooms and dorms were so focused upon the facts of life that we momentarily forgot that we were living in a world that is probably doomed.

Then came the heartless assassination of Linda and Groovy in New York's derelict Lower East Side, irrefutably demonstrating the innocent stupidity of our belief that we could build a good life in society's dead cities: the slums. And we finally understood the naïveté of our efforts to play at being proletariat; and we figured out why blacks and Hispanics wanted to get out of the ghettos in which we were so anxious to be accepted.

While we were shouting "Power to the People!" we had to face the slow rage of impoverished blacks and Puerto Ricans who de-tested weirdos and hippies, who—as far as they were concerned—were belittling and destroying all the symbols of middle-class afflu-ence which they desperately sought. In our precious ghettos, minorities—brutalized into brutality—were attacking Diggers' free stores and clinics. "Peace" became an absolutely ridiculous slogan to offer people whose pain and deprivation were so massive that they could only respond to us with rage. So we broke off diplomatic relations with the Third World: we had failed to bring the vast population of abused and hungry people into our cause. Now we were outsiders in both suburbia and the slums. We had become social revolutionaries without a revolution.

Within our own subculture things were steadily falling apart. Longhair proprietors of head shops were high-power business people. The Fillmore East ushers were called the Gestapo by rock fans of 1969. And our superstars had gradually shocked us with their views on women (groupies), on money (capitalism), and on politics (fanatics or bleeding-heart liberals).

Arising out of our self-centered idealism were creatures who looked like hippies but were something terrifyingly strange. We first caught sight of them at the Altamont festival. In the presence of the Hell's Angels we recalled some of that deep, silent terror we had of brutes when we had been kids on the playground. And in the scuffles and glares of anger we began to recognize the sheer helplessness of our great superstars-superstuds, who—unlike Moses—could not turn back the sea with a single command so that we might safely stride toward the magic of their music as we had at Woodstock and Monterey. The brutalized crowd, cowering from the erratic blasts of motorcycle bravado, reminded us of old movies about juvenile delinquents, gang wars, drag races, and street rumbles: antiques that we were certain had been left behind in the world of our older brothers. But here they were again: rising like rubber models in a science-fiction film—dinosaurs!

And when finally the pool cues began to beat back some enormously fat, nude boy, we knew it was all over for us. We were dying again . . . dying of our massive appetite for humanity. The same act of faith that had directed us to imbibe unidentified potions also directed us to engulf and to absorb huge, fatal doses of derelict humanity. The ranks of alienated, antisocial psychopaths were being naively taken into the generation's main flank where they were then turning into mad dogs and destroying those who befriended them.

We were frightened by the mirror image we saw among the crazies. And so we said to ourselves: they are mad but we are not mad. "But if you were not mad," said the Mad Hatter, "you wouldn't be here!"

No, we insisted, we were not mad! Admittedly, we had been compromised by middle-class education and morality. But we were certain that we were not as crazy as straight people said we were. We had simply broken out of the psychological enclosures of our parents' stifling social order, and we had found a new premise for being both politically critical and creatively sane. Surely that was not madness!

But the crazies recognized us by our isolation, our contempt for authority, our abhorrence of tradition, and our self-description as *freaks.* We had dropped a couple of caps of this or that, and we had become the symptoms of the dementia of which they were the disease. None of us could tell the difference between us anymore: not even the hippies themselves and not the press, which had been searching for four years for the ultimate embodiment of the young maniac, long-haired freak Devil.

So it was inevitable that Charles Manson would appear in our image and enact his insane rituals in our behalf. It was even inevitable that we would then embrace him, defend him as a comrade and care about him, since it was our prime virtue and our prime weakness to love and to protect the foundlings of our parents' cruel society.

The confusion of dream and reality became song in John Lennon's first solo album. We have never tried to separate our individual fate from the fate of our generation—that was an intrinsic and retrograde aspect of our notion of tribalism. So for Lennon, it seemed as if everything had been lost. "The dream is over," John sang.

Behind him John left all our heroes, our sojourn in the confusing and beguiling mysteries of orientalism, our belief in absolute evil (Hitler) as clearly opposed to absolute good (Kennedy), and even our music (Elvis, Dylan, the Beatles).

In his song, Lennon bid farewell to all our dreams. John's moment, like our moment, is gone, and now it is difficult to remember exactly what it was that we believed with such utter conviction.

Four dead at Kent State. Countless invalids who barely survived the drugs sold to them on street corners. Countless more who did not survive. And yet we must fashion from our disillusionment some kind of memory. As a friend of mine said to me when I was lamenting the passing of an era: "Yes, it's true, there were some really terrible things that went down in the sixties. But just think of it—just think what a bright, strong light it took to cast such a dark shadow!"

IN EUROPE

After 1972, I withdrew from the world of popular culture. By that time I was so closely identified with an obsolescent counterculture that magazine editors and book publishers wouldn't even consider a proposal of mine that didn't promise to be another best-seller about the rock scene.

Success is a prison. You are supposed to specialize and you are supposed to repeat your successes. If you want to undertake a major change in your life, professional people consider you erratic and irresponsible, and the general public becomes suspicious of you. I had been researching pre-Columbian culture for a number of years, but nobody—with the exception of one underground newspaper that didn't pay writers—would publish my pieces on the subject. The editor of the national music magazine for which I had been a long-time contributor wouldn't even discuss my writing interviews or record reviews for his classical music section. He wanted me to stick to pop material. Even the radio stations for which I produced talk shows insisted that I continue my familiar format. I tried to accept this advice, and as a result I found myself writing a series of obituaries for the pop stars who were dying and for their dying world.

I believed that I was a writer of some talent, but no one knew or cared about the youthful fiction I had written when Anais Nin had been my mentor. I started submitting short stories to publications and receiving polite notes informing me that I should stick to the stuff for which I had a reputation. My agent at the William Morris Agency bluntly told me, "It would be a different matter if you were a *literary* writer, but since you're a pop journalist, it's very hard selling your experimental prose."

Clearly I needed to get away from my own success. I needed to find the courage to decline offers to take part in pop projects that didn't interest me, even if the alternative was poverty. I had to get rid of the reputation that had taken almost ten years to build. So I began submitting proposals for work related to popular culture, but with a slightly different focus from what was expected of me. Eventually I began to get assignments from a couple of major newspapers —the *Chicago Tribune* and *The New York Times*— to interview people in film.

While I was shuttling between New York and Los Angeles, chasing movie stars and directors, I noticed that airplanes were filled to capacity with young people in backpacks, hippies en route to Europe. It was the era of charter flights, youth fares, and Icelandic Airlines. A whole generation of Americans had suddenly rediscovered the "grand tour," and young men and women, teachers, professors, and college students on vacation were shipping out by the thousands.

When I first visited Europe in 1967, I had taken along one of the famous guidebooks that promise the whole world for a couple of bucks a day. It wasn't long before I realized that these books were not produced for *travelers,* but for tourists who wanted to spend twenty-five minutes at the Vatican, sixteen minutes in the London Tower ogling the crown jewels, and one day in Paris, principally at the Moulin Rouge and the Eiffel Tower. It seemed to me that there was a great need for a different kind of guidebook: one that addressed itself to the spirit of adventure and cultural curiosity that was typical of a new breed of traveler. In 1971 I submitted a three-page proposal for such a book, and within ten days I heard from Eugene Fodor, publisher of the best series of travel guides in America. I became coeditor with Fodor of the book I had proposed. Suddenly the whole world was mine. For four years I constantly traveled, with temporary home bases in various European cities: Paris, Brussels, London, Kuşadası. Finally I leased an apartment in Zurich for a couple of years.

Eugene Fodor was an exceptional collaborator. He was highly cultivated and intelligent, and extremely cordial. I recall the afternoon he flew to Vienna in order to have lunch with me so we could discuss the third annual edition of our guidebook. We had a table reserved on the outdoor terrace of Zachers, but when we arrived the headwaiter took one look at my jeans and turned a lighter shade of pale. Fodor was absolutely outraged by this kind of priggish behavior and demanded to speak to someone in charge. Fodor handed the manager his card, and the manager instantly realized the awkwardness of the situation: people in tourism never cross swords with people who write travel books! There were so many apologies that the situation became both sad and comical.

But other incidents during that time were not as humorous. I was in one of the communist nations of Eastern Europe when *The New York Times* ran a story suggesting that Fodor Guides was a cover for CIA agents who posed as travel writers in order to infiltrate unfriendly countries. Such an allegation is the sort of thing that one does not refute. Those who believe it will continue to do so no matter what you say, and those who don't believe it don't require an explanation. I imagine that there are still people who feel certain that I was a spy for the CIA.

A colleague of mine then was Stephen Birnbaum, who has subsequently become a major force in the travel-writing industry. Steve

Jamake Highwater in Munich, West Germany

often encouraged me to aim for higher goals as a writer. "You don't want to be a *travel writer* all your life, do you?" he would insist.

A few years after I left Fodor, when my writing began getting favorable reviews and a few awards, Birnbaum and I had a drink and talked about our time at Fodor. When we had started, Steve and I had both been unfamiliar with the procedures of publishing. We had had no idea how the major houses treated writers. So Steve asked me if publishing "real books" with major houses was different from my experience at Fodor. I smiled with amusement. "To tell you the truth," I confessed, "it wasn't until I published my first book with another publisher that I realized something very surprising. For years magazine publishers had revised and rewritten my work to such an extent that I was surprised to read it when it was printed. I assumed that that was the way it would always be for me as a writer. So during my years with Fodor I wasn't surprised by the fact that I didn't see a final, revised manuscript or a set of galleys for any of the books I produced for them. I just handed in the manuscripts and hoped for the best. Then, when I did a book for Little, Brown, I was absolutely delighted to discover that my editor conferred with me on the slightest change in my work and requested that I personally make revisions."

"That just proves what I told you all along," said Birnbaum. "The only thing crazier than being a travel writer is being a spy for the CIA."

ZURICH LOVE LETTER

I am a committed fan of the Zurich Tonhalle Orchestra, which I heard two or three times a week for almost two years while living in Switzerland from 1973 to 1975. Those performances constitute some of the happiest recollections of my Swiss residency. There were also less pleasant memories, like the time an outraged neighbor knocked at my apartment door on my very first night in town, informing me that in Zurich decent people do not make a lot of noise and disturb their neighbors by flushing their toilets after ten o'clock! I cannot keep it a secret that I had a love-hate relationship with Switzerland. I often complained about the Swiss passion for order, which made me long for a bit of litter in the streets. Fortunately, in the arts generally and in music particularly, much that is best seems to overflow from the soul of Switzerland.

There was never really a full-time conductor of the Zurich Tonhalle Orchestra during my days in Switzerland. I was able to hear a schedule of music conducted by Karl Böhm, Rudolf Kempe, Gennady Rozhdestventsky, Ferdinand Leitner, Kyril Kondraschin, Josef Krips, Jean Martinon, Erich Leinsdorf, Georg Solti, Antal Dorati, Carlo Maria Giulini, Lorin Maazel, and many other conductors (some, alas, now gone). Unlike the practice at festival performances, however, these great musicians did not bring their own polished orchestras with them, but came for a sojourn in Switzerland, where abundant funds for the arts permitted them to lavish time on rehearsing the Tonhalle Orchestra. Erich Leinsdorf found the cosmopolitan ski-village atmosphere of Zurich so pleasant that he stayed for weeks and presented a series of nine or ten concerts of the music of Mozart and Stravinsky—an intriguing and curiously effective repertory. Krzysztof Penderecki lingered long enough to rehearse and to perform an entire program of his music.

The soloists are every bit as impressive at the Tonhalle as the conductors. The dour-looking Swiss have heard Benedetti Michelangeli (who actually showed up for his recital), the Quartetto Italiano, Pierre Fournier, Rudolf Serkin, John Browning, the Guarnieri Quartet, and numerous young European instrumentalists on their way up. The programs were stupendously diversified and daring by comparison with concert repertories in London, Rome, Paris, and New York. I heard a rare peformance of an Ernst Krenek work for soprano and orchestra based on Robinson Jeffers's *Medea.* I heard a great deal of Beethoven, Mozart, and Mendelssohn as well. But I also got to hear John Cage, Olivier Messiaen, Mauricio Kagel, Hans Zender, Arthur Honegger, Morton Feldman, Witold Lutoslavski, and many of the other composers whose music was rarely heard even in Manhattan when the courageous Pierre Boulez was the director of the New York Philharmonic. I cannot claim to know if the people of Zurich liked experimental music, but I can say for certain that they listened to it. They didn't boycott concerts devoted to twentieth-century composers, and they didn't scamper for the exits when

a bit of serial music was heard in the hall. They listened as intently
to Cage as they did to Bach. Then they applauded as only the Swiss
tend to applaud—not very loudly and not very long. As for me, I
would stagger out of the elegant hall and go across the street to the
edge of the lake from which the Alps rise into seven jagged summits.
Rarely was I less than thrilled by the music, let alone the night and
the swans and the eternal mountains.

THE DIRTIEST
WOMAN OF BARCELONA

Mary asked me if I wanted to see her tits and popped them out before I could react.

"It mucho illegado in España," she Spaniardized politely while looking down admiringly at her breasts, "to showing de boobsies in de stage, señor ... making me feel deprimeda ... terrible bad to dressed up me boobsies when de hombres coming me to see all de ways."

Mary Mistral, the dirtiest woman of Barcelona, smiled nicely and pushed her considerable frontage back into its narrow setting of rhinestones and sequins before dashing back to the stage of the tiny

Mary Mistral

El Molino Teatro, where she stars in a little show that is billed:

¡¡Estreno del Super Show!!
¡¡Ay Que Doctor!!
¡¡Mujeres Hermosas, Humor,
Picardía, y Mucho Sexy!!

When Señorita Mistral returns to her immense and cruddy dressing room, I ask a frank question: "As a Spanish woman, how do you feel about virginity?"

Mary lurches, apparently caught between fainting and hitting me. "Ay! Señor!" Then, blushingly, ". . . please not being deerty with de señorita! Madre de Dios!" And she turns abruptly, frantically swishing her huge headdress, which she holds in her hand like a fan. But even in the face of Ms. Mistral's huge indignation, I remain a true journalist who dauntlessly asks the most ridiculous and stupid and personal questions. "Do I take it," I say politely, "that by your reaction, Ms. Mistral, you believe in virginity?"

"Señor!" she shouts in a blaze of self-righteousness, tugging majestically at her G-string and giving me a full blast of her Joan Crawford eyes. "Huf course! I am a Spanish womans!"

I make quickly for the door as the torrent of Mary's profanity rolls out of her mouth like a dialogue balloon in a Tijuana comic book.

The show at El Molino is part of a tradition that goes back to nineteenth-century Barcelona, which at that time was the most notorious port in the world. The live sex show was invented here in Las Ramblas—a wide avenue filled with bird and flower venders. While ladies in New York were still covering their ankles, Barcelona was up to its pretty thighs in excess. In the old capital of Catalán you could indulge yourself and live to tell about it. In principle, if it felt good you could find it and do it in Barcelona. In 1975, much of that madness was gone, but the Ramblas was still a full-time sideshow where you could find absolutely anything in the realm of sex. Toward the bay the wide promenade gets more and more crummy, with proliferating stalls, people, bars, and cafes. The little streets that twist off from the Ramblas into the utter darkness of the night are as safe as a Hollywood set—something out of a Maria Montez movie: buildings hung with laundry, cobblestone lanes covered with litter, resounding shouts and cries, haunted old women sitting in doorways, and at least two million stray cats. In these alleys are the weirdest little bars and dives on earth. But despite their cloak-and-dagger appearance, they are harmless.

For years the Franco government "exiled" undesirables to Barcelona. But after the dictator's death, Barcelona ceased being a "prison colony" and became a thriving cultural center. Today, all that remains of the bad old days is Mary Mistral, who stars at El Molino in an endless succession of little shows that seem to have tumbled out of a Fellini dream. Two hundred oversize mamas with their spit-and-polish boyfriends are stuffed into the little theater every night . . . hanging off the tiny balcony, eating *galletas,* and having a marvelously loud time. They shout insults at Pipper, who plays the fag; they adore the girls with their drum majorette costumes and tremendous breasts; they hate and love the incomparably mincy Johnson, whom they bring on with a song they all know by heart and which they warble in huge voices. When Johnson finally swishes onto the cramped stage with its tons of tinsel, the crowd screams with affection and loathing, hurling sexist insults at him and then waiting anxiously for Johnson's stupendously bitchy retorts. Then they howl with pleasure.

At the climax of the scene, the tinny septet in the pit coughs up a colossally tuneless showstopper and Mary Mistral strides into the pink lights. The back of her glittering gown is cut well below the cheeks, and she flashes her plentiful ass. Fannies are permitted in Spain, but breasts are mucho illegado! The audience goes completely crazy while Mary blinks her enormous artificial lashes . . . playing Bette Davis on her three-foot cigarette holder and parading her fantastic bod.

El Molino preserves an authentic bit of grand debauchery. It is the kind of cabaret that Christopher Isherwood must have seen in old Berlin. And Mary Mistral epitomizes everything that is most fascinating about the theatrics of decadence. She's a triple-barreled combination of raw sexuality, lunacy, and innocence. Whether she's tilting her hips at the balcony, crouching to mutter a perfect obscenity to a guy in the front row, or crossing her eyes and flashing her taillights, Mary is a first-rate example of a rapidly vanishing breed.

In the Bodega Bohemia

She understands the absurdity of her role and brilliantly mixes humor and unrestrained sexuality . . . making us recognize the preposterous image of the long cabaret tradition of the female sex object.

Mary may be a dying species, but she's in her prime compared to the old biddies at the nearby Bodega Bohemia, where a different kind of trashiness reigns. Here is a nonstop talent showcase for the fading swans of Spain's once great nightclubs. The Bodega is sometimes known as the Florence Foster Jenkins Memorial Club—and everyone from Marcello Mastroianni to Truman Capote has dropped by to sit in astonished silence while ancient ladies looking like Bela Lugosi in drag hobble to center stage and belt out a song.

These wrinkled refugees from the classic plays of Lope de Vega have retained very little voice, but they still have a great deal of wit as well as a peculiar madness. The old woman at my table at the Bodega gets up and waddles toward the piano. After conferring briefly with the maestro, she almost sings "Granada." Then she almost plays the accordion, and then she caps off her performance by doing a few crotchety bumps and grinds while peeking coyly over her handkerchief.

After abundant applause, she slinks back to her chair and pants until someone hands her a drink. She takes one ladylike sip and then empties the glass in one gulp.

"Trashy?" she mutters toothlessly with a wise grin, when I ask her about the bawdy history of Barcelona. "My dear young man, you don't know what the word means! Now," she smiles as she drifts off into memories, "in my day we were *really* trashy!"

TURKISH JOURNEY

The year is 1972. The ship *Ege* ("Aegean") surges through the Black Sea, which is filled with glowing, white gelatinous creatures called medusae, peculiar apparitions that have barely ascended from the level of protoplasm. This lovely tide is also infested with tons of human debris, scattering in our wide wake as we throb out of the harbor of Istanbul—slicks of oil, plastic bags, newspapers.

I am ill. I must have eaten something that has made me dreadfully sick. My head spins and I must constantly go out on deck for fresh air. Along the coast, as we sail eastward away from the Golden Horn, the immaculate plains gradually change into a strip of low, isolated peaks, sparsely foliated and darkest green. We are now free of the harbor's refuse, and yet the water is utterly lightless and life-less except for the masses of gelatin umbrellas that cover the entire surface, ebbing like formless specters in the dark waves. The Black Sea has none of the bright azure illumination of the Aegean, none of its sunny clarity and calm. It is a mysterious and somewhat fearsome expanse of dank water.

The fresh air does not help my head. Even after ten hours of sleep, I cannot seem to shake the fever and nausea that exhausts me. Per-haps the Black Sea voyage will be a good place for recovery, and so I make the most of my leisure: relaxing and sleeping. In the mornings, in the first light, I sit on deck and write in my travel journal. The movement of my pen and the flow of words comfort me.

The ship _Ege_ is old and she sighs and groans in misery as she lunges through the dark water. She is one of several ships that make the run between Istanbul and Hopa, a tiny town in the east of Tur-key near the Soviet border. The Hopa Express retraces one of the an-cient sea routes of the Orient, although today its prime importance is providing access to one of the final outposts between Turkey and the Soviet Union.

Sinop, the first of several stops on the three-day cruise, is disen-chanting: a modern, small port without any visible tradition or his-tory. After the exoticism of Istanbul and the history visible everywhere along the Aegean coast of Turkey, where I make my summer home—Troy, Izmir, Pergamum, Kuşadası, Ephesus, Priene, Miletus, Didyma, Söke, Milâs, Bodrum, Marmaris, Antalya, Alanya—Sinop is a terrible disappointment. When I creep back aboard, exhausted and pale from my slight exploration, my Turkish friend Zaferyap frowns with deep concern. "Ah," she intones in the doleful manner typical of the Turks, "you will die. Yes, I know it; you will die. And then all of my enemies will say that I took you to the end of the world and left you there to perish!"

I assure Zaferyap that I will survive, even this voyage to what is indeed the end of the world, for the eastern territory of Turkey is more desolate and alien than almost any other place on earth. In the days to come, I realize that very few urban Turks have ever ventured to the distant places that I will visit with Zaferyap. There will be times on our arduous journey when no one in our party will be able to comprehend the dialects spoken, when finding food and lodging will become supremely difficult.

At five in the morning the *Ege* glides silently into the harbor of Giresun. I pull on my clothes by the light of a candle. The stop at Giresun is to be brief. When I reach the deck I find Zaferyap patiently awaiting me. It is still very dark, and the other passengers, who do not have cabins, are huddled in blankets on the lower deck. They momentarily peer at me—the crazy American who in the middle of the night noisily descends the ship's clanking gangway, stepping into the silhouetted city where pale lamps vaguely illuminate the tiny streets.

Without delay we start the ascent to the ancient *kale*—the ruined Pontine citadel and the tomb of Seyyit Vakkas, whose military prowess won the old city, then called Karasu, from its Byzantine rulers. As we climb the steep streets a few early risers stare blankly at us. A man in an alcove, barefooted and capped, kneels in his first prayers before beginning the day's fast in honor of the month-long holiday Ramadan, which has just begun. In the gutters, bands of spotted dogs sniff through the garbage while a solitary man with a thrush broom collects the garbage and dumps it into his donkey cart. Enormous gray and black birds, called *saksagan,* hop menacingly with loud cries from rooftops to the ground, where they fight noisily over bits of debris. Everywhere is the heavy odor of fish and cats.

Women with veiled faces begin to descend into the streets. Zaferyap greets them, as she pants heavily from the difficult climb. She is a very large woman with no taste for hiking. But she is a good friend, and she follows along after me no matter how perilous my adventures. When Zaferyap has recovered her breath, I take her small, round hand and help her climb to the top of two crumbling remains of the *kale* that has brought us to the summit of the little town in the night. As the sun makes its way into the sky, the view is stupendous. Far below, down the steep descent of the hill, the Black Sea gradually turns purple in the first light. The hills along the coast twist fantastically into separate points, outlined by the wide fissure of brilliant sunlight that the dawn tears across the enormous, dark sky. Hundreds of feet below us, in the murky sea, fishermen cast

Zaferyap and Jamake Highwater

their nets from small boats that make large circles in the motionless water, as battalions of seagulls sweep upward suddenly, with a great cry, filling the newly lighted world with a million flapping wings.

The ship *Ege* calls out to us with a single, resonant hoot. We must hurry down the long trail in order to reboard her before the seven o'clock departure.

I lock myself in my cabin and instantly collapse from exhaustion and fever. In my dreams Zaferyap is whispering anxiously and I hear the vague jangle of the steward's passkeys. Then suddenly I awaken and sit up in bed with a startled shout. People are in my cabin.

It seems that Zaferyap had gotten it into her head that I had gone off to my room to die. When she saw me, near nude in my bedroom, she was mortified. She is a traditional Turkish lady, so she turned crimson and covered her face as she stammered and retreated from my cabin. The steward and I had a good laugh, and I asked him to tell my humiliated friend that I would soon join her in the dining room for lunch.

My buoyant mood lasted only until I stood up. Then the illness came back. Zaferyap had gone to great trouble to prepare what the Turkish believe to be a curative meal: yogurt dissolved in water, plain rice, and an absolutely revolting herbal tea. I did my best to eat the food, but soon I had to excuse myself. The captain and his officers nodded politely as I passed their table, certain that I was a terrible greenhorn with a legendary case of seasickness. "I am not seasick!" I insist as they smile. "I swear I was already ill when I came on board." The officers smile again.

The captain of the *Ege* is a very refined gentleman. To me he is exceptionally hospitable and utterly charming. To others, I notice, his manner is rather superior, reflecting an attitude of nobility typical of Turkey's upper classes, whose assets are the same in most non-industrial nations: wealth, education, civil authority—especially the kind that is associated with a uniform.

In the Turkish pecking order, women occupy a very low station. It is only recently that women have begun to attain rank in government—and only in Ankara. It is difficult to come to terms with the vast differences between the Asian and Western views of rank and gender. And though I hoped to understand Turkey, I often found myself confounded and dismayed by what I saw there. Zaferyap, for instance, was always treated with great respect by men. But the tribute was not given to her because she is an important woman, but because she is educated, has civil authority, and comes from a family of wealth. In fact, my persistent impression was that Turkish men accept Zaferyap *despite* the fact that she is female. She was often addressed as *efendi,* which means "sir"—there being no such formal title for addressing a woman.

The ship *Ege* sits calmly in the harbor of Trabzon. Zaferyap and I accept the invitation of the captain to join him for a farewell luncheon. A table is set on the promenade deck, and there we sit in the brilliant sunlight, having an extraordinary meal prepared by a cook from Bolu, a province renowned for its classical Turkish cuisine.

The crew rushes to work when we briefly tie up at Trabzon, and the captain excuses himself briefly in order to discuss a problem with the first mate.

Meanwhile, Zaferyap and I have made our travel plans. We will disembark at the next port, Rize, and after spending the night in the town, we will hire a car and driver and take the road inland to the monastery of Sumela, about thirty-three miles southwest of Trabzon. When the captain rejoins us he announces gallantly that he has delayed our departure from Trabzon so that the short trip to Rize will take place during the sunset. And so, while Zaferyap and the captain and I talk about voyages and adventures and drink black tea at a tiny table in the long light of the late day, the ship *Ege* makes her calm silent way along the coast. The sea slowly turns bronze as the sun falls behind the hills, and the dimming light twists into the mountainous shoreline and then fades gradually to black. The engines of the ship become silent. The voyage has ended just as the sun vanishes, leaving first a glorious burnished horizon and then, very suddenly, an utter and gigantic darkness.

We are anchored now in this becalmed blackness, illuminated only by a distant string of shoreline lamps and the tiny halo cast by the yellow lights of the ship. There is no wharf or harbor at Rize, and so we are obliged to anchor offshore in the deep water at some distance from the town. Over us, in the moonless sky, appears an unbroken festoon of stars.

The captain wishes us a warm farewell. "You have reached the end of the world," he says with a smile. "Few travelers come here. But if you are looking for a Turkish adventure, you have come to the right place. Be well and be safe."

We strain to see in the vague yellow light as we climb down the clattering metal gangway that hangs loosely against the hull of the old ship. I jump into the black belly of the large wooden barge that will carry us to the shore, as it rocks and bucks in the dark sea. A group of children tumble down the steps as Zaferyap tries to make the four-foot jump from the gangway to the barge. Finally she makes her move and we all reach to catch her very large figure. There are no benches or railings on the little boat, just the hollow, oily wooden hull—affording no seat for Zaferyap except the very large pile of our luggage. There she sits like an overstuffed pillow, looking rather worried when the gas engine down in the small, luminous pit of the barge chugs to life, and we glide into the appalling darkness—surrounded by nothing but the enormity of the black water and the opulence of the sky, where lights increase fantastically as the *Ege* falls back back back into the night.

Next morning, our driver and his cousin quickly pack our luggage and picnic lunch in their bright purple 1965 Chevy while Zaferyap and I finish our breakfast of toasted rolls, goat cheese, and tea. The journey to the monastery should take only an hour, but the new road, as always, has not been completed, and it is piled with debris. All along the Turkish highways loom the wrecks of battered buses, trucks, and automobiles—grotesque souvenirs of horrendous accidents, with splintered windshields and twisted metal frames.

Our drivers have a carefree attitude about driving, and I can detect, despite her efforts to conceal it, that Zaferyap is nervous. We must constantly take detours from the new highway, chugging along the old one-lane dirt road, which is a solid procession of trucks and which skirts cliffs with thousand-foot drops. Zaferyap's pretense of calm vanishes, and she gapes at me in panic each time we swerve toward the brink. I try to reassure her that we are perfectly safe. Our drivers, I insist, are experts.

The Zigana Mountains rise suddenly around us: furious geological upheavals, jutting upward in every direction, solid rock that looks like it was tossed into chaotic heaps by demented giants. Between the rock, incredibly, the pines rise perfectly serene and straight.

We park in a tiny cove dug into the face of the cliff and prepare to hike the rest of the distance to the Sumela monastery. It is the most important Byzantine structure in the region, but is now abandoned and crumbling in the hollow of a sheer cliff some one thousand feet above the valley where we have parked. We must climb to an altitude of almost four thousand feet by way of a rugged little path. Twenty-five minutes walk from the road, the rocky landscape suddenly changes: small waterfalls, garish ferns, and a huge chasm of luscious foliage. Wooden bridges dangle over boulder-filled streams; the water froths over the crags, turning white. The highway and the world seem far away now. Here the animal tracks are still fresh. I am surrounded by a greenness that I have deeply missed since arriving in this arid region of Turkey. For the first time in days my head clears of the fever and I feel well.

Now we are climbing toward the face of a huge weathered cliff that rises into a sky so brilliant that I cannot see any trace of the monastery that is supposed to be carved, quite literally, into the naked surface of this natural fortress. About three-quarters of the way to the top is a small, ruined chapel. I come alive in this thin mountain air, and I have outdistanced my friends, who lag far behind, puffing for breath. While I wait for them, I pick my way carefully to the brink of a finger of stone that juts over the sickening height. The valley is so far below me that it seems to be a river of color, slowly moving under clouds. When I look up I catch sight of the monastery for the first time, perched like some fantastic fairytale castle on the summit of the mountain, clinging to the cliff. The five-story original structure is now a three-tiered ruin, oozing with a perpetual flow of lime and water. The frescoes, however, have endured—tucked under a huge overhang in the cliff that protects them.

When Zaferyap sees me on my rock perch she begs me to return to safer ground, which I do reluctantly. The young guardian of the monastery has heard our approach and comes to greet us. Twice daily he walks four miles to and from his village to show the monastery to the handful of adventurers who come to see it. He is the sole protector of this vast architectural treasure, which he regards as something of an unkempt eyesore in the otherwise beautiful landscape ... decorated, as it is, with Christian saints and symbols that haven't the slightest significance to him. He confides that he cannot imagine why people bother to come such a long distance to see such a Christian wreck. I assure him that he is the guardian of a very great historical monument, but he is unimpressed. "We have had Alexander the Great. We have had the Phoenicians. We have had Romans and Hittites and great sultans of the Ottoman Empire. Why should I be impressed by an old building?"

We must climb ninety-three steps to a locked wooden door perched in midair along our perilous pathway. The guardian unlocks this gate with a huge key. On either side of the steep wooden stairway that scales the cliff are the remains of an aqueduct that once brought water to the monastery from nearby springs.

I am wandering through the dank rooms. The ancient frescoes are badly defaced—slashed, gutted, and embroidered by several centuries of Islamic graffiti; most of the saints depicted have had their eyes gouged out. Zaferyap is deeply disturbed by the vandalism. "Ah," she mutters, "the Christians ... the Ottomans ... they were all savages! They destroyed and they destroyed ... everything had to be remade into their own image. That is a bad way for people to live."

Touched by her statement, I wander off by myself. At the cliff's edge I am utterly alone. Every sound in the river valley below rises like music; water, wind, the sigh of branches and grasses, and the song of birds. And all around me are the slowly fading pastel frescoes: saints with their faces filled with bliss, reenacting a sacred drama before a vast but desolate landscape, raising their arms and beseeching pity from the trees and the cliffs, weeping with eyeless eyes.

The pass over the Zigana Mountains is a rift between two landscapes. We leave behind the lush damp green of the coastline and climb steeply upward through misty forests that grow out of walls of gray rock. Suddenly the land changes again to the high, arid Asiatic plains covered with tough, thorny scrubs and clouds of yellow dust.

Driving is extremely difficult. Zaferyap squeezes into her corner of the seat and clenches her fists and closes her eyes. We must stop occasionally for rest. She is pallid and speechless. While I am taking pictures of the curious houses of the district with their stacks of corn husks piled high around a central stake, she makes an effort to talk to our drivers and explain her concern for our safety. But the men have turned surly and are clearly annoyed to be criticized by a female. I am angered by these difficult men, but when I try to speak to them, they pretend that my Turkish is incomprehensible.

"What can we do?" Zaferyap sighs. "We are miles from a town where we could rent another car and get rid of these fellows, and they know it."

When we get back into the car, the driver immediately roars up the road, hardly giving us time to close the doors. The mountains drop behind us as we soar upward, and we find ourselves approaching the sheerest roadside cliffs that I have ever seen. Not even the spectacular cliffs along which they built roads in the Spanish Costa Brava compare with the horrendous drops along the roadsides of eastern Turkey.

The highway is not really wide enough for two lanes of traffic, but regardless of the danger, our driver thunders along, the music from his cassette player howling. I keep recalling the twisted wrecks we have seen strewn like crushed beer cans along the roads of Turkey and feel certain that at any moment a truck will vault around a curve and smash into us, sending us and our car into empty space.

At times the world disappears entirely from our windows as we rise to a summit. Now I am resolute. I order the driver to slow down. He ignores me. Momentarily we drop into a tiny valley and I am overjoyed to see trees and grass and solid land again. But the valley is hardly more than a dip in the unending ascent of the road, and we begin at once to rise out of the glen at a terrible speed.

Suddenly I see a peculiar sight. It is a wooden hut just beside the road. It stands there in the middle of nowhere, and in front of the hut is a very old man with a white beard and a cap. I try to comprehend why he is waiting there in this desolate region and why, just as we approach, he rises slowly from his position on the ground and waves us on with a little white flag. Later, when I tried to recall that moment, I couldn't understand its meaning or even be sure it really had happened, but I shall never forget the expression on the man's wrinkled brown face as he gestured to us, as if beckoning us onward toward that terrifying ascent. Then, as suddenly as he appeared, he was gone.

It was only a moment later, as we took a wide, hairpin turn, that there was a terrific burst of energy and sound. I recall seeing something out of the corner of my eye.

It was the front wheel, the entire front wheel of our vehicle, flying off, bounding up an embankment, ripping through the trees, and then tumbling back down toward us, crashing with a sickening thud into the door beside me, and finally flying high into the air and falling . . . down into the valley hundreds of feet below us.

The car went out of control. The axle skipped and hissed and plowed along the road, sending up huge sparks and smoke and making a dreadful noise. For a moment we swerved furiously to the right, and then we began to spin gradually around as we headed straight for the edge. There was no chance to leap out or try to save ourselves, though the automobile seemed to be moving in slow motion. Strangely calm, I simply sat and watched the small trees at the edge of the cliff moving in on us as the world began to disappear on both sides of the car and all that was left was an enormous empty sky.

Then we stopped.

Zaferyap had fainted. The drivers were hysterical as they scrambled out. I got out numbly, pulling the half-conscious Zaferyap after me as carefully as I could, afraid of unbalancing the automobile, so close was it to toppling over the cliff. Something compelled me to glance down. Just beside my foot was a sheer drop of fifteen hundred feet.

We were still in a daze when a bus stopped to offer us help. Our drivers continued to curse and pray and apologize, but we heard none of it. We ignored them as we loaded our luggage into the back of the bus and climbed aboard. The drivers were jumping up and down outside the bus, beating on the window beside us, shouting that we owed them several hundred Turkish lire. I simply stared at them through the glass. The bus pulled away and I gazed back at the automobile dangling over the edge of the cliff.

When we came to the spot where I had seen the old man, I could see no trace of him. Perhaps, I told myself, he was on the other side of the road. Perhaps he had never been there at all.

Zaferyap reached into her purse for a cigarette. It was Ramadan, and smoking was prohibited. Angry brown faces turned toward us as Zaferyap lit her cigarette. "To hell with you," she muttered. "I'd drink a pint of whiskey if I had it!"

Then she looked at me with an expression full of confusion, and suddenly we both burst into laughter.

"Well," she exclaimed as she chuckled, "you said you wanted an adventure!"

Our laughter was so filled with the joy of still being alive that it slowly swept the entire bus, and soon even those severe brown peasant faces began to light up with smiles. Then, as our bus rumbled safely down that perilous hill, people at the side of the road stared up at us, for we left behind a wide resounding wake of laughter. Now everyone on the bus was roaring with uncontrolled mirth, tears streaming down their faces.

THE MUSIC FESTIVALS:
RANSOM WILSON

Zurich was my home base during 1973 and 1974, while I wandered around Europe visiting museums, concert halls, opera houses, libraries, archives, historical sites, film festivals, music festivals, universities, theaters, spectacular landscapes and seascapes, and the homes and studios of writers, painters, and composers. It was the most intense possible education. Of all the many adventures of those years, the ones I relish most were my times at the festivals. I spent an entire year visiting every major film, music, theater, and visual-arts festival: Cannes Film Festival, Berliner Festwochen, Edinburgh Festival, Festival van Vlaanderen (Flanders), Salzburg Festival, Bayreuth Festi-

Ransom Wilson

val, Vienna Festival, Holland Festival, Bath Festival of Music, Glyndebourne Festival, Helsinki Festival, Festival d'Avignon, Bach Festival (Madeira), Spoleto Festival dei Due Mondi, Biennale di Venezia, Bergen Festival, Drottningholm Opera Festival, Montreux Jazz Festival, and many more.

One of my most vivid memories is of a program of contemporary Norwegian chamber music I attended one evening at the Munch Museum in Oslo. I wandered through the empty galleries, gazing at the profoundly disturbing and fascinating pictures of Edvard Munch while distant music shimmered through the air all around me. And there was also the bright summer afternoon on the terrace of the Grand Hotel in Cannes, where everyone was anxiously awaiting the arrival of Diana Ross for the film festival awards. When a huge limo rolled up to the hotel, the flash bulbs burst and reporters rushed forward while a mob of fans threw flowers and confetti. The bewildered black woman who stepped out of the car was not Ms. Ross.

I also remember sitting in the unmatched solemnity of the lobby of the St. George Hotel in Edinburgh, watching Maestro Carlo Maria Giulini sipping coffee while a world-famous soprano loudly bitched to her companion. And I recall my much anticipated visit to Berlin's famous Philharmonie in Klemper Platz, where I was to hear Herbert von Karajan conduct the massive Seventh Symphony of Anton Bruckner. Unfortunately, the architectural maze designed by Hans Scharoun was so complex and the ushers were so uncooperative that I didn't manage to locate my seat until after the maestro had walked onto the stage. While extended applause greeted him (and long before the music began), an usher held up her arms with typical German authority, announcing that I could not take my seat—which was only four rows away—because von Karajan forbade anyone to enter the hall once he was on stage. So much for Bruckner.

At the Flanders Festival, I heard flutist Ransom Wilson perform for the first time. In the immense Flemish cathedral of the medieval town of Ghent, a crowd of short, round burghers and their wives had assembled in the rainy northland night of Belgium to listen with considerable stoicism to the Cologne Chamber Orchestra playing the music of J. S. Bach. Conductor Helmut Mühler-Brühl turned to the stupendously inert audience and raised his brows as he lowered his torso in a bow. He then returned his attention to the orchestra, flipped a few pages, and nodded to the young American flutist, who lifted his golden instrument and began to play, as only Ransom Wilson can.

After the concert, the cathedral emptied as people went off to have their half glass of wine at the Staathaus, which is one of those huge medieval wedding cakes in concrete, the facades swarming with a multitude of carved Jesuit grooms (but no brides).

I stayed behind and trudged through the Flemish program notes until I recognized a quote from Jean-Pierre Rampal. "Ransom Wilson," it more or less read, "is one of the most brilliant flutists I have encountered in many years." So I wasn't half mad with Flemish influenza after all. There were others who heard what I had heard!

I stumbled into the drizzly street feeling a bit more rational at having such good company as Rampal in my opinion of Ransom Wilson. As I passed one of the countless little *pommes frites* stalls that are stuffed into every crack of the Belgian thoroughfares, I thought I recognized the conductor of the Cologne Chamber Orchestra standing quite alone, eagerly pushing large quantities of fried potatoes and mayonnaise into his rotund face. "Very nice concert," I said. He burst into a big smile, and after wiping the grease from his hand, patted me fondly on the shoulder.

"Listen," he lamented politely, "after such a concert on such a night like dis, we got to going mit da bus Gott knows how much kilometers all ways back for Cologne! Here I'm standing in da rain half collapsed mit da fatigue and nothing to eating all day! So I am happy dat you loved our music!"

And Ransom Wilson? Where, I asked, had he been discovered?

"Ahuh, the kid mit da flute. Him I found in New York where he goes back now. One concert and goody-bye. Dat's life, my friend, dat's life. Have a *pomme frite.*"

THE LONDON THEATER

When it comes to the theater, London and New York seem to work the opposite sides of the street. If New York is up, then London is rather down. In the fall of 1975, I was in London, where a marvelous theater season was under way. At the head of the list of current triumphs was Tom Stoppard's tour de force *Travesties,* while the biggest flop of the London season was easily the Royal Shakespeare Company's dreadful *Jingo.*

Between these extremes were about eight other plays, some premieres and some revivals. The best of the revivals was the Brecht-Weill musical *Happy End,* which worked very well in a new English translation, proving that the British definitely have the knack when it comes to the presentation of slightly tarnished ironic comedies.

Another set of excellent revivals provided an overdue blessing for the writing of Joe Orton, the playwright who was murdered by his roommate in August 1967 at the age of thirty-four. For a long time, the popularity of Orton's curious and deadly comedies was looked upon as the attraction of camp, but by 1975 critics and audiences had begun to recognize Orton's power. John Lahr, who wrote the authorized biography, sums up Orton's peculiar gifts: "In showing us how we destroy ourselves, Orton's plays are themselves a survival tactic." There is in all of his plays an indulgence in gratuitous violence and cruelty unleashed upon the passive, numbed characters by other characters who are cunningly aggressive. The fact that Orton himself was the victim of a hatchet murder isn't beside the point, for his life ran parallel to his message. He was the first playwright in England to dramatize the psychopathic style of the sixties—that restless, ruthless, single-minded pursuit of satisfaction—transformed by drugs, political fanaticism, and rock music into violence disguised as love.

All of these observations aren't superficially implicit in Joe Orton's theater, which abounds, instead, in amusement, seeming innocence, and an utterly nonchalant and steadfast kind of violence. The underside of his comedy is where the horror show lies hidden.

His last play, *What the Butler Saw,* is probably his best work, and its revival was extremely successful in London. I knew the play from an earlier off-Broadway production in New York that a couple of friends and theater collaborators of mine, Richard Barr and Charles Winward, had mounted with a good deal of affection and style. *Entertaining Mr. Sloane* is less finished as theater, but its revival focused on several of the play's previously neglected virtues, thanks to brilliant performances by Beryl Reid as Kath and Harry H. Corbett as her brother Ed.

The theme of exploitation, of getting what you want at absolutely any cost, was perfectly unfolded in *Entertaining Mr. Sloane* by director Roger Croucher. Reid and Corbett, both of whom fancy the visiting young Mr. Sloane, played by Kenneth Cranham, use treachery to get what they want, and eventually even sacrifice the life of their aged father (played by James Ottaway with great skill).

Beryl Reid starred in the 1969 film version of *Entertaining Mr. Sloane,* though she is far better known to American audiences for her great success as the lead in the film *The Killing of Sister George.* On stage at the Duke of York's Theatre, she tackled Orton's lines with enormous insight; she was helpless, coy, and hilarious in her role as an English spinster with the hots for a young man. As the brutality of the guest is gradually revealed, she doesn't let it hinder her unmotherly affection for him. And when it becomes clear that her brother also has plans for the young man, she willingly makes a pact with him whereby they can share the boy's company. They insist upon sampling the young man's charms even after their elderly father accuses Mr. Sloane of murder, a confrontation that ends with the father himself being done in by the sexy young psychopath. That such a plot can keep an audience laughing for two and a half hours is perhaps the perfect tribute to Joe Orton's strange view of our world and its goings-on. It seems clear that the Ortonesque combination of wit and horror, innocence and cunning, is bound up in a special quality of the British theatrical sensibility.

Without its bitchiness and its flawless performances by a highly polished cast, *A Family and a Fortune,* by Hulian Mitchell, from the novel of I. Compton-Burnett, would have been very nearly as boring as the novel itself, the author of which justified this drama about a family and its problems over an inheritance with these words: "There are far too many books written about sex and far too few written about money." The play is an attempt to put things right. The plot is anything but straightforward: a fairy-tale fortune descends out of nowhere on an impoverished but highly refined family. The year is 1901, and we are given a full dose of all the stereotypes of British family tragedy, including the everlasting preoccupation with class distinctions, breeding, family solidarity, and Victorian mannerisms.

The tedium of the play gets so colossal in the final scenes that on the night I attended, Alec Guinness, playing brother Dudley, broke up while trying in earnest to deliver some of the play's sublimely meaningless axioms. He brought the play to a complete halt, while his fellow actors tried desperately to wipe the smiles from their faces.

Guinness was wasted in a role he could not turn into a credible character. Anthony Nicholls, playing brother Edgar, was a bit more blessed by the playwright. But the plum of the evening was handed to Margaret Leighton, who romped through a preposterous role as a lame dowager with such talented determination that I was glad to listen to her, even though I didn't believe a word she was saying! As one might expect from a British family drama, everything turned out all right in the end, and the elderly audience went back out into the London streets with that smile of satisfaction that used to accompany a reading of Rudyard Kipling.

If *A Family and a Fortune* suffers from saccharine, *No Man's Land* is a triumph of sweet oblivion. It was the first new play since 1969 from the familiar and diabolical Harold Pinter, who had signed out of the theater in that year with the premieres of *Landscape* and *Silence,* leaving us with little more than Pinter as television and film writer and stage director. *No Man's Land* not only brought Pinter back to the theater, but may very well be one of his best plays. It provides all the familiar and devastating Pinterisms: the eloquent and poetic versus the violent and vulgar. *No Man's Land* is about two stately gentlemen named Hirst and Spooner, who are utterly lost in time and space. Spooner provides refined and endless conversation that staggers dizzily but cannot articulate the commonplace. In contrast, there is the somnambulistic Hirst, whose capacity for the commonplace is rarefied to the point of nightmare. The only other characters are two thug-hirelings of Hirst's, named Foster and Briggs, whose unsavory statements imply violence and fear.

No Man's Land glorifies indeterminacy, a quality in the early Pinter world that always suggested that his characters were running an incredibly complex maze. Act one of *No Man's Land* abounds in convolutions, fragmentary sentences, and colliding monologues. Act two suddenly and effectively becomes far more explicit, involving a mysterious retelling or creation (one cannot be certain) of earlier years, during which Hirst (now a successful though sterile writer) and Spooner (an unsuccessful poet) were the bright young literary hopes at Oxford.

Foster and Briggs, the polished henchmen of the subplot (Hirst's valet and secretary), were performed with hair-trigger ferocity by

Michael Feast and Terrence Rigby.

But the most startling impact of *No Man's Land* arose from the stupendous performances of John Gielgud as Spooner and the late Ralph Richardson as Hirst.

Gielgud epitomized the slightly tattered, vulnerable loser whose enormous self-justifications flooded the first act in an almost nonstop monologue. Meanwhile, Ralph Richardson, stoical and in a lordly trance, generated a monumental self-righteousness. This air of disdain and vanity was achieved by Richardson with absolute economy, a fact which was all the more amazing when it is realized that he spent almost the entire play seated stiffly in an armchair. Twice in the first act he fell (perhaps drunkenly) to the floor with such choreographic deliberation and control—like the action in a Noh play—that Pinter's world of irreality was instantly and perfectly affirmed.

No Man's Land is brilliantly perplexing—though somewhat more literal and polemical than Pinter at his obscure best. In this drama, even the title itself is a bit of a giveaway, and what's more, Pinter doesn't hesitate to inform us exactly what he intends by the title:

> Spooner: *You are in no man's land. Which never moves, which never changes, which never grows older, but which remains forever icy and silent.*

Approaching a play by Tom Stoppard is like reaching for a rainbow—for all its colorful impact, you can't touch it. Stoppard's world is governed by laws that don't touch the rest of us. To say that *Travesties* is a play about Lenin, James Joyce, and the dadaist Tristan Tzara in Zurich during World War I utterly misses the point, suggesting a historical drama that doesn't have the slightest resemblance to the uproarious, intellectual, and strongly theatrical offerings of *Travesties*.

However, simply outlining what *Travesties* is about from a structural standpoint might be impressive, but would once again fail to come to terms with its achievement as theater. What Stoppard has done, in part, is to paraphrase *The Importance of Being Ernest* at the same time that he has injected large doses of Joycean methodology—

like the question-and-answer sequence that follow's the "night town" episode in *Ulysses* (while Bloom and Stephen are urinating in the garden). In *Travesties* Stoppard uses this kind of scholastic interrogation of Tzara by Joyce as a brilliant device for filling in the history of dadaism, which happens to be just one of the arguments squeezed into the play's comical shape. At the same time that Stoppard's ploy allows him to deal with dadaism, it also turns into a delightful send-up of Joycean method.

Stoppard also employs a fictionalized "historical" style that makes absolutely no effort to keep things in their actual chronology. This cunning manipulation of time doesn't stop with history: Stoppard also uses "time slips" (as he calls them) within the play itself, whereby a scene is repeated two, three, or four times in various dramatic styles: realism, surrealism, vaudevillian farce, and so on. Within this nonhistorical framework, characters suddenly break into song and dance without the slightest motivation and then, as abruptly, start again from the top of a scene and repeat the sequence in quite a straightforward and realistic manner.

The initial effect of all of this mannered playwrighting is very funny—even those who don't have the slightest idea what is going on philosophically are guaranteed more laughs per minute than in any other recent comedy. There are also laughs for specialists: for those who have lived in Zurich and know its icy people and its provincialism and have had drinks on the terrace of the Odéon Café, and for those who know their Oscar Wilde and the works of Joyce. There is also an astonishing sublevel of debate that studiously explores the place of the artist in civilization, the validity of nonliteral art forms, and (Lenin versus Tzara) the contrasts between revolution in art and revolution in politics.

> Tzara: *The odd thing about revolution is that the further left you go politically the more bourgeois they like their art.*

Lest it seems that Stoppard has wantonly cooked up a Swiss stew with communist, Joycean, and dadaist trappings, one should note that there's a tangible historical basis for the whole pastiche, which, though hardly essential to the fun, nonetheless adds enormously to the drama and to the philosophical questions raised by the play.

Joyce, Lenin, and Tzara were residents of Zurich during World War I, though they were hardly aware of each other's existence. For the most part, *Travesties* is presented through the fevered imagination of its principal character, Henry Carr, who is no less historically real than the other main characters of the play. But contrary to Stoppard's Henry Carr (Stoppard makes him the British consul general of Zurich), the real Mr. Carr was an actor who joined an acting group called the English Players. None other than James Joyce was the business manager of the fledgling group. The first play presented in Zurich by this group was Oscar Wilde's *The Importance of Being Ernest*! So it all begins to hang together.

"I conjured up an elderly gentleman still living in Zurich"— Stoppard explains in discussing Carr—"married to a girl he met in the library during the Lenin years, and recollecting, perhaps not with entire accuracy, his encounters with Joyce and dadaist Tzara."

All of my efforts, however, to applaud *Travesties* have hardly touched upon what made it easily the best play of the 1975 London season. Clearly, my pleasure in the play was greatly indebted to a superb production by the Royal Shakespeare Company and to the direction of Peter Wood, the staging of music numbers by William Chappell, the decor of Carl Toms, and the lighting of Robert Ornbo. The most applause went to the exuberant cast, headed by John Wood, who played Henry Carr with such energy that one didn't know whether to send him roses or vitamins! Robert Powell was a dashing and racy Tzara; John Quentin was a suitably brash and boorish James Joyce (holding together a long and hilarious sequence performed entirely in limericks). Meg Wynn and Beth Morris swished, swooned, and sashayed with exclamatory perfection as Wildean ladies Gwendolyn and Cecily. John Bott greatly helped the first act as Carr's manservant, Bennett, while Frances Cuka carried the role of Lenin's wife on appropriately proletarian shoulders. Only Harry Towb as Lenin seemed conspicuously miscast, not so much because he failed to animate the role as because the role itself lacks animation, and also because Towb's presentation was in a style entirely at odds with that of the rest of the cast.

It's the old Henry Carr who ends *Travesties,* as he pumps away at a cigarette and slouches around in his robe and nightcap. "Great days. . . . Zurich during the war. Refugees, spies, exiles, painters, poets, writers, radicals of all kinds. I knew them all. Used to argue far into the night . . . at the Odéon, the Terrasse . . . I learned three things in Zurich during the war. I wrote them down right here. Firstly, you're either a revolutionary or you're not, and if you're not you might as well be an artist as anything else. Secondly, if you can't be an artist, you might as well be a revolutionary. I forget the third thing."

Blackout and curtain.

BACK TO SOHO

It was the end of 1975. I was growing weary of Europe and I missed America and wanted to go home. But home had drastically changed. What had once been a depressed downtown area was in the process of becoming Soho. The apartment that I had detested for years was now in the midst of a district undergoing a cultural renovation so vast that at first hardly anyone could figure out what was happening.

People had been illegally living in industrial lofts for years. I had lived in a loft near the Public Theater until a building inspector evicted me. Lofts provided an abundance of open space for a minimum rent—and in Manhattan that combination was a dream for people in the arts. About the time I returned from Europe, collectives of six to ten tenants were buying and converting loft buildings in a rundown district south of Houston Street, between Lafayette Street and West Broadway. Under the proarts administration of Mayor John Lindsay, the lofts had finally been legalized.

These were fantastic days. I remember walking out of my apartment and often seeing such noted artists as Laurie Anderson, Merce Cunningham, Edward Albee, Louise Nevelson, Bob Indiana, John Cage, Lucinda Childs, and Bob Wilson. Experimental theaters had been producing work for almost a decade in industrial spaces among the littered streets. The Performing Garage on Wooster Street, where Richard Schechner's theater work *Dionysus in '69* had attracted audiences into a veritable slum, was just one of several ventures that predated the Soho boom. On weekends you could see performance artist Laurie Anderson playing her violin on a street corner while wearing ice skates atop a melting block of ice. Leo Castelli opened his gallery on West Broadway. The restaurant FOOD became the first gathering place for local artists. If you lived in Soho you knew that something important was happening there—but outsiders were not aware of it.

One afternoon I bumped into Robb Baker on Spring Street. I had met him when he interviewed me at *The Chicago Tribune* for the 1968 publication of *Rock and Other Four Letter Words*. We became friends, and eventually I talked him into relocating to New York.

"We're starting a new paper," he told me. "Want to write for it?"

"How about classical music editor," I suggested.

"Why not," he said.

The newspaper was called *The Soho Weekly News*. Robb was the managing editor in charge of arts and entertainment, and Michael Goldstein was the editor in chief. For four years, Robb and Michael allowed me to do my weekly column, as well as special features, with complete freedom. I wrote for shares of stock in the paper. Among my associates were James Beard, Annie Flanders, John Calvin Batchelor, Don Whyte, John Perreault, Marcia B. Siegel, Paul Krassner, Allan Wolper, Arthur Knight, Mona Da Vinci, William Harris, and a good many other accomplished journalists and critics.

After four years I quit. I walked into the office one day and felt out of place because I didn't have roller skates or pink and blue hair. *The Soho News* had gone punk. Shortly thereafter it went under. While it lasted it was the only American journal charting the Soho art scene—a community of artists and an explosion of experimental activity often compared to Paris of the 1920s.

Spaces like The Kitchen were becoming vital alternative centers for performance artists, composers, and video artists. The musical life of the time was equally diversified and challenging. I used to go to five or six recitals, operas, concerts, and dance performances a week and still found time for a film or two as well as a couple of visits to galleries. I vividly remember how difficult it was to get press passes from publicists. "What paper do you write for?"

"The Soho News."

"The *what?*"

By 1976 they were at our doorstep. Suddenly *The Soho News* had great cachet. All the doors of the uptown citadels of culture opened to us, but I often returned to the downtown centers where new and emerging artists could be seen and heard. I recall the evening I reviewed one of Jessye Norman's first American performances of Mahler songs at the Brooklyn Academy of Music (BAM) when Lukas Foss was the conductor of the Brooklyn Philharmonia. Jessye and I became friends, and I had the opportunity of writing about her brilliant rise to fame. Not too many years later, when the impetus behind the Soho explosion was diminishing, I bumped into Jessye at a Lucinda Childs program at BAM's Next Wave Festival—which had become a new center of avant-garde energy in America. Jessye was friendly with Lucinda; she had also performed with Ransom Wilson; she was working on a piece with Bob Wilson; and she and I were old friends. We were all connected and it was exceptionally exciting.

At Gregg Smith's annual Christmas Eve party, all of the members of the Gregg Smith Singers and countless other musicians crammed into the living room of Gregg and Roz Smith, embracing friends they hadn't seen since the prior Christmas and singing carols at the top of their voices. In the late sixties, Gregg and I had had great fun collaborating on a highly experimental electronic album with producer John McClure at Columbia Records. Out of the experience, we became close friends with a strong interest in extending the range of vocal music. As a result, for several years Gregg's group had performed one of my aleatoric choral works ("This Is the Word") on national tours.

At the Smith Christmas party, Ned Rorem sat in the kitchen, surrounded by a circle of admirers. Lukas Foss chatted with me briefly before bounding out the door. "One day I must set something of yours to music," he insisted for the tenth time in ten years. Then he dashed to a taxi, en route to the airport and a conducting engagement.

In a crowded corner, composer Gerald Busby and I talked about our mutual friend Virgil Thomson, who wasn't able to attend the party. Virgil had been the inspiration for the style of my music writing at *The Soho News*. I recall meeting him at a dinner at his apartment in the Chelsea Hotel. It was the first of numerous visits during which I shouted questions into his good ear, and he filled the hours with vivid and outrageous tales of Picasso's unhappy dinner with Gertrude Stein, of Hemingway's awkward literary confrontation with Stein, and of all the other luminaries and upstarts of the great Paris years of the Lost Generation. During my second meeting with Thomson he inscribed a copy of his book *Virgil Thomson by Virgil Thomson* to me: "For Jamake and the beginning of a long friendship!" At eighty years of age, that was more than optimistic! But that inscription is now almost a decade old and he's still going strong.

Another annual Christmas party that I attended with great pleasure was held at the Central Park West apartment of Lucy and Robert Mann. Bobby's fellow members of the Juilliard String Quartet would drop in; along with an array of writers, musicians, and scholars. Every year, there were performances of chamber music for the guests, who sat on the floor and sipped wine. *The New York Times* executive editor Abe Rosenthal and his wife, Ann, who lived upstairs, chatted with Pinchas Zukerman, while Elaine Pagels, Liz Diggs, Sharon Olds, and I had an exuberant conversation. Bernard Malamud sat rather solemnly with his wife on a couch, graciously declining to say much of anything to anyone.

I met Bobby Mann in 1981, during my years at the Aspen Institute, where I had crossed friendly swords with Mortimer Adler on a series called *Six Great Ideas,* produced and hosted for public television by Bill Moyers. Later, Bobby and I collaborated on an arts festival at the glorious Baca Grande campus of the Aspen Institute, located in remote southwestern Colorado.

These were good days, a time when I won the regard of those I most admire and realized some of my goals as an artist and a person. They were happy years, though not without their complexities and uncertainties. I had finally made a name for myself. But the name wasn't my own. It belonged to my foster father. So while friends and professional associates looked on with a great deal of concern and astonishment, I legally changed my name back to its original, pre-adoption form. And I quickly learned that many people are very suspicious of change.

These Soho years were a turning point for me. I had written articles for many major publications. I had sometimes twisted my language and even compromised my ideals to fit the formats of magazine and newspaper editors. I had also learned a great deal about writing from them. Now, at last, it was time to produce my own work in my own way and with my own name as a byline. Soho was the birthplace of that rare self-realization and liberty.

Wilhelm Reich, the brilliant and bizarre psychiatrist, was talking one day about the unwilling "enemies" of the middle class: creative artists, intellectuals, students, and illiterates. Reich found this totally illogical, since the same middle class professed to admire art, education, and innocence.

Reich's hate list of outsiders evokes a question: Where do these threats to the middle class live? Few are aware that artists, intellectuals, and students, like other minorities, are confined to a sort of ghetto existence.

Newsweek, in a review of Martin Duberman's fine book *Black Mountain,* about the experimental college, makes this observation: "The book is devastating in its implications about how America drives its true innovators underground." The predicament, however, is not truly American, neither predominantly nor exclusively. A quick look at the world's major cities establishes the fact that few have a stimulating and permissive bohemian quarter where creative people can live and work. The exceptions include, in Europe, Paris's Left Bank (now a tourist attraction), Munich's Schwabing (also a tourist and student district), London's Chelsea and Notting Hill, Barcelona's Ramblas, and Antwerp's Conscience Square. In the United States, there are San Francisco's North Beach and its adjacent port-community of Sausalito (both, however, havens for tourists), Boston's Beacon Hill, Chicago's Old Town, Portland's Reed College district, and New York's Greenwich Village, Soho, and Tribeca.

These are floating communities inhabited by "island" people— separate, alienated, compelled by creative energies. Alone because they will not be part of the herd, "poor" because they do not compete in traditional financial arenas, "nonpolitical" because they cannot believe in politicians, and "unsuccessful" in conventional terms.

Artists' ghettos are not the romantic havens that tourists make of them. The artist-inhabitants, like most minorities, are either trashed by or excluded from the media, reminding us that history is the story of the ruling class. And yet it is this artistic minority, virtually excluded from establishment art history, that may be the most active in creating that history.

Outcasts tend to gather into protective groups, in districts where rents are low and neighborhood morality is not too restrictive. In such places, no one is alarmed if a painter's lights are on till five a.m. or if a musician's stereo jars the midnight hour. And folks who sit out among the garbage cans on hot summer nights are not more than passingly amazed by a young man and woman hauling trash out of their tiny flat where they are fast transforming squalor into slum-elegance. Hardly anything fazes these neighbors, not the fanatical young bearded window-gardener and not the many couples of mixed colors and genders.

Currently the most renowned resurrected slum is New York's Soho (short for "south of Houston Street"), a recycled zone that has rapidly grown into a working community and an artists' district. It was originally a semi-ethnic, semi-industrial neighborhood where light manufacturers of pasteboard boxes, office furniture, textiles, and hardware products coexisted with a few block-wide churches and half blocks of Italian and Puerto Rican demighettos. The pavement was cracked and gutted. Manhole covers were missing. Water incessantly oozed from fire hydrants. And under multiple coats of industrial paint, the architectural beauty of the looming old industrial buildings was almost missed by the occasional passerby. In the summer of 1973, New York's Landmarks Preservation Commission had declared Soho a historical site, "because the area contains some of the most unusual, pre-Civil War, cast-iron architecture in the country."

In the early days of Soho, there was a constant churning of machinery, and soot flew out open windows and chimneys. Trucks rumbled to and fro, and at four in the afternoon, the thousands of people employed in the various lofts poured into the streets. And then they were suddenly gone, leaving nothing but the night and a few abandoned cats and a couple of drunks who had wandered from the Bowery into the enormous silence between the dark buildings.

In those days, if you glanced up at two a.m., you might have seen a few lighted windows on Wooster Street or on Greene Street. These were the secret lodgings of artists, people who lived with the persistent fear of New York's loft dwellers: discovery by a building inspector and subsequent eviction.

Industrial lofts are not normally zoned for residences; therefore, artists, writers, and dancers are expected to use the low-rent lofts for business only and somehow manage to lease additional space for living. Obviously, artists live where they work—and can barely afford that comfort—so it became traditional for them to live illegally in their lofts, using every conceivable ploy for hiding their beds and disguising their other household fixtures.

As the number of loft dwellers proliferated, a steady grumble began to be heard in Soho. People were tired of not answering their doorbells lest they find a city inspector at their step. They were also running out of inventions to camouflage refrigerators, stoves, and bathtubs (all illegal furnishings in industrial lofts). Someone finally voiced the obvious question: Why not legalize loft dwellings in Soho?

The legal fight lasted a couple of years. It's an indication of Mayor Lindsay's dedication to the arts that the Soho legalization program got through the grind of government, permitting, under very specific safety and health regulations, lofts to be used as residences by painters, sculptors, filmmakers, and dancers only—specifically, the kinds of artists who require the most precious urban commodity, space.

The result of that small zoning victory slowly evolved into a community in which the inhabitants tried to avoid the destructive intrusion of tourism and commercialism. In the late seventies, loft dwellers became as paranoid about being taken over by tourists and uptown people with the money to pay the increasingly high rents as they had once been about being evicted by building inspectors. Their concern was justified: few people in the arts can afford to live in Soho today. Nonartists with high incomes and tastes for novelty and flair have descended upon Soho, making it into just another ritzy bohemia. The situation is a perfect paradox. As artists improved the district, the community necessarily attracted art patrons first and, eventually sightseers and kids looking for weekend kicks. It took about five years for the newest art ghetto to become a high-fashion, high-rent district, as had Greenwich Village before it.

The rise of the number of art galleries in Soho has been prompted by the art boom of the seventies, when art increasingly became a commodity. Initially, the avant-garde prevailed. Dilettantes opened junk-eloquent showrooms with a fashionable minimum of spit and polish. But soon uptown art hoodlums got the scent and began to open galleries with a distinct air of slickness. Then followed row upon row of international boutiques, expensive restaurants and bars, and all the other trappings of a full-scale art mart.

Many of the art people have moved away, leaving only those who scored enough success to retain their lofts—which could be bought for fifteen thousand dollars in 1973 and now bring in as much as thirty times that! The new and young arrivals from virtually every city in the world have either had to come with a substantial family subsidy or have looked for new derelict districts to transform into art ghettos. Their efforts have largely been concentrated in Alphabet City—a very depressed area around Tompkins Square, between Avenue A and Avenue C. Given enough time, even this pathetic wasteland will probably become a high-rent district.

I will never forget the fledgling days of Soho: West Broadway in

1972. It was already getting dark and the small crowd across the street was disbanding, leaving poet Ralston Farina and his friends, who were doing a "time piece" in chalk on the sidewalk. The lights in the factories have gone out, and the workers are pouring out of the buildings, trampling Ralston's frail handiwork, hustling noisily between the unhurried artists whose jobs are never finished. On the whole, the old population seemed to coexist easily with the art invaders.

Now it is dark again. Fire escapes, hydrants, and debris. This could be the Soho of fifty years ago except for the luminous halo of upper windows. All along the back streets, above the barred factories, windows are filled with light and plants and the outline of the island people engaged in their own time and space, fashioning and fabricating the ideas and the images of tomorrow's todays.

MUSIC ON VIDEO
AT THE KITCHEN

At The Kitchen, Robert Ashley's *Music with Roots in the Aether* made music nice to watch. Even then, in 1977, I had the strong suspicion that such experiments with music video could evolve into a big industry.

At The Kitchen, where I had seen a series of music videos, some of the music was a lot more interesting to see than to hear. And that—perhaps—is exactly what this series of video portraits of composers produced and directed by Robert Ashley is all about. It visualizes the music-making process of a certain set of composers (most of them associated with the West Coast): David Behrman, Philip

Robert Ashley (center) with Alvin Lucier and Anne Koren

Glass, Alvin Lucier, Gordon Mumma, Pauline Oliveros, Terry Riley, and Ashley himself. The use of remarkable, single-take videotography, intriguing color, and excellent stereophonic sound provides an entirely original, landmark approach to "packaged" musical entertainment, but what seems to me most impressive about this project is the manner in which the traditional production of interviews and musical performances has been realized.

At first, viewers may get the impression that Ashley and his talented cohorts are involved in a bit of self-indulgent post-Dada exploitation: frankly, I was put off by the Philip Glass interview (the first one I saw), in which a gang of kids munch and jabber away in the background while Glass and Ashley talk about *Einstein on the Beach* and several other subjects that interest me sufficiently to make me annoyed by the intrusion of the children. (And I don't care if this approach is trying to tell me that artists shouldn't take their ideas too seriously.)

Seen by itself, the Glass package—an hour of talk shot in a glowing white studio setting with kids galore and another hour of music shot fairly traditionally—might seem like a lot of tricky ploys trying to disguise a very low-budget educational TV show. But taken as a whole, the fourteen hours of *Music with Roots in the Aether* establish a whole new attitude about music and video, and eventually one begins to recognize the validity of the metaphors with which Ashley surrounds each composer. Nothing makes this quite as clear as the amusing, intriguing, disturbing, astonishing, and finally revelational interview with Pauline Oliveros, who speaks plainly and insightfully about "art putting you in new situations" while her friend arduously transforms her into somebody's plastic mother with the use of makeup, a wig, a flashy dress, and all the other weapons of middle-class fashion.

Terry Riley's seriously articulate interview is, by contrast, set in the Northern California foothills and romantically builds an idyll around Riley's vague orientalism and his San Francisco transcendentalism. The interview with Alvin Lucier is a delightful bit of theater in which the flatness of the image (a masonry structure), a canoe, a couple of dancers, and Lucier in a fishing outfit combine with resonant silences, persistent tone loops, and the sound of the fishing reel clicking out miles of minutes. During all of this, Lucier is talking (and, of course, his stuttering adds measurably to the sonic hesitancy of the whole piece) and evoking the natural environment of sound in music. "After all," he says, "in-in-in Java those pe-pe-people were really using th-th-those gongs and drums to pro-produce the most f-f-fundamental sounds which surrounded them."

Sometimes the imagery was far more impressive than the sounds. Gordon Mumma was well served by camera operator Philip Makanna, who produced a remarkable ambiguous machine during Mumma's "Schoolwork." While the composer sat in a deserted amusement park playing a crosscut saw with a bow, the camera coyly approached one of the gigantic, light-decorated joyrides and, with soft focus, transformed it into just the kind of undescribable experience that Mumma's music was entirely unable to provide.

Musically, the series was most attractive in the works of Philip Glass and Terry Riley. Everybody seemed comfortable with the notion that these seven composers have something in common. I'm not so sure. They are, so to speak, postserial and post-Cage and post-modern in their interviews—but I'm not certain that their actual music consistently upholds the views they express. Ashley, at one point during Riley's interview, suggests that what all seven of his composer friends have in common is the production of music from an internal world, coming out of few concrete influences and yet all possessing a kind of personal, meditative character. But if those are the principles upon which composers secure roots in the aether, then I can think of a good many artists (some of whom Glass mentions) who are perhaps more significant as examples of this sort of composition than some of the composers presented by Ashley; namely, Alan Hovhaness, who started the whole minimalist trend years and years ago, Harry Partch, and Steve Reich, not to mention the vocal mannerisms of Carl Orff, the pop innovations of Magna and Mother Mallard, and the tradition of gamelan music in Bali and Java, and even the curious redundancy of the film scores of Nino Rota.

Ultimately it is unimportant whether Ashley's friends represent more a circle of personal affinities rather than a substantial musical trend. The video series depends far less on the concepts of the music than on the elaborate imagination of producer-director Ashley. He has created the first alternative to the phonograph record and audiotape. He has also created an atmosphere in which music becomes intimate rather than alien to us. Music video has a future. It recreates the people who create the music.

COLLECTING
RICHARD KOSTELANETZ

Richard Kostelanetz and I met at frenetic 1960s New York parties now and again. The two of us would sit in opposite corners talking determinedly to editors from whom we couldn't get change for a quarter, let alone a book contract. Sometimes in desperation Richard and I would walk away from the people and lean heavily upon each other. Richard was one of the very few people I knew then in Manhattan who had a glimpse into the future of the arts. And it was our mutual preoccupation with the future rather than the ever-stoned present that made us friends, though friends who have actually seen very little of one another. Our acquaintance began and evolved al-

Richard Kostelanetz

most entirely on the telephone, making our friendship the sort of conceptual event that is perfectly suited to the futuristic cosmos of Richard K. Usually the telephone would ring at about three in the morning when I was busily casting short spells at my typewriter.

"How are you, Richard?" I would ask, realizing at once that it was Kostelanetz.

Then in rapid-fire, informative prose Richard would relate all the notable events of the publishing world, capping off his commentary with a few questions about my own work. Then very abruptly he would sign off, leaving me in the nighttime silence with the peculiar feeling that an apparition of immense power had just flashed past.

By the early 1970s the act of thinking was considered old-fashioned. Kostelanetz was one of the rare people of the period who made absolutely no effort to deny the fact that he very often indulged in thought. There were, of course, other thinkers, but they were usually concerned with how much of the eternal past was being lost on the mass of unwashed adolescents of our time, whereas Richard was thoughtfully constructing an intellectual vision of the everlasting future. His ideas were so perfectly on target that his writing was widely ignored by those who were blissfully untouched by thought and widely criticized by people who apparently had not read anything he had written. Yet Richard Kostelanetz was then and remains today one of the most articulate and influential spokespersons for the avant-garde. I recall, back in the period when Erica Jong was writing poetry, she once asked me with considerable urgency why it was that Kostelanetz didn't admire her work. I never ceased to be surprised by the variety of people who sought his approval. The range of Richard's influence was quite staggering in those days.

Whenever a major statement of the state of the arts was needed by *The New York Times* it inevitably fell upon Kostelanetz to provide it. It was, in fact, his very generous and insightful review in the *Times* of my first book, *Rock and Other Four Letter Words,* that brought us in touch. Richard was the only person who had the slightest notion of what I had attempted in that visual book. His review was a major breakthrough in my career. It was also Richard's book about John Cage that brought that composer into international focus. And in those convoluted "countercultural" days, it was Kostelanetz's numerous, decisive, and pioneering anthologies that introduced and celebrated the most neglected and significant experimenters in the various arts who might otherwise have had no recognition whatsoever. In this way, Kostelanetz was a precious bridge between those who live in the present and those who live in the artistic future.

During many of our late-night telephone conversations, Richard and I used to wonder what had become of those very great writers of the twenties, thirties, and forties whose richly inventive works had been celebrated by intellectuals. We often tried to grasp how it was possible for the most important writers of our own day to be producing books for people who normally read nothing but best-sellers. "There are only two kinds of success," he would say, "the kind that is successful and the kind that isn't."

Then Kostelanetz would lament the death of the avant-garde.

If, as many people suppose, the future of art is not avant-garde, then Richard K is living in the past. But I am very much inclined to believe that as always Richard sees something that is not yet visible to the rest of us. While all the world seems to be screeching to a tremendous minimalist mindlessness, Kostelanetz is unfalteringly dashing into the unexpected future. It was René Char who said, "For those who are walled up, everything is a wall." But for Richard Kostelanetz, everything is an open door.

A NIGHT AT THE OPERA: CATHERINE MALFITANO AND SAMUEL RAMEY

It is the fall of 1977. We are sitting in the cool midafternoon atmosphere of a mirrored and paneled room in the New York State Theater at Lincoln Center. The panels are antique Chinese screens, the carpet is deep green, and Samuel Ramey is talking about his life in opera.

Suddenly the tall French doors open and a dark, attractive young woman makes a sweeping entrance, smiling as she slips out of an elaborately embroidered black coat and coming into our corner where she multiplies our numerous reflections in the many mirrors of this handsome room. Her name is Catherine Malfitano.

Catherine Malfitano

Samuel Ramey

"I'm late, but it has been one of those truly operatic days, if you know what I mean. The simplest little comment becomes a big aria and everything else turns into a tragic scene." She laughs as she sits next to Samuel Ramey and taps him gently on the cheek. "And what are you two discussing so seriously? No, don't tell me: let me guess. *Football!*" she laughs.

"As a matter of fact," young Sam says in his resounding basso, "we are talking about dramatic truth in opera."

"Oh, my," Malfitano sighs, "I suspect that there is no end in sight to that discussion. It's something that all of us who are involved in opera are constantly asking ourselves—what is operatic acting? What I mean is this," she continued, settling at once into the conversation, "does operatic acting have to be treated in some special way from, let us say, acting in a play?"

For a moment the two opera stars look at one another, as if each expects the other to clarify the question. But neither speaks. So we sit in the silence of the mirrors and the Chinese screens.

These two attractive young singers are part of a new breed of operatic performer—technically skilled beyond the expectations of prior generations of stars, unusually concerned with the merits of the productions in which they perform, rather than using the stage as a gray setting for their colorful egos, and uniquely intelligent and artistically knowledgeable. There was a time when people talked about poodles, bon-bons, and opera singers in the same breath. One had about as much expectation of a lively conversation with a singer as with a Louis XIV doorknob. Opera singers were famous for only two things: grand gestures and trivial minds. If they weren't singing they were usually eating or having a tantrum. If they weren't making a grand entrance they were walking out on a contract. They relied on largeness: in voice, in physique, and in the size of their name in the printed programs.

"It is possible that prior generations of opera singers had idols whom they admired and copied, but I don't think that is true of young singers today," Malfitano explains in her direct, serious manner. "I admire the Callas voice—but I never saw her and I don't think Sam did either . . . did you? . . . no, you see, neither of us ever saw her perform. And so we depended far more on other things we grew up with, like the actors and dancers we saw in the theater and in film and on television."

Catherine Malfitano grew up in Manhattan and attended the High School of Music and Art and the Manhattan School of Music. The vital influence on her early music training, as well as her principal vocal teacher, was her father, concert violinist Joseph Malfitano. Since her professional operatic debut with the Central City Opera in the summer of 1972 as Nanetta in *Falstaff*, she has become a special kind of singer with a unique dramatic capacity in the standard operatic repertory and an abiding interest in contemporary operas. Already in 1977, she had performed at most of the great opera houses in the world, and her performances had been nationally broadcast on public television's *Live from Lincoln Center* series. The *Detroit Free Press* probably summed up the opinion of most critics when it stated that "Catherine Malfitano could sing a stock market report and make it sound dramatically interesting. She uses her voice like Garbo used her face."

Bass-baritone Samuel Ramey was born in Colby, Kansas, where he became interested in music during his high school years. He studied at the School of Music of Wichita State University and spent his summers at the Galtinburg Music Festival in Tennessee and at the renowned Santa Fe Opera. Moving to Manhattan, Ramey became a national finalist in the 1972 Metropolitan Opera auditions, and the next year he made his debut with the New York City Opera, with which he was closely associated during the golden years of that opera company. Since his remarkably rapid rise to international stardom, he has sung in all the major opera houses of the world, has been featured on numerous recordings, and frequently appears on public television. Ramey has a distinctive style of his own, although, as *Time* magazine put it: ". . . it is easy to see why Ramey is fast filling the shoes and cape of the late Norman Treigle."

"There are very few opportunities," Catherine Malfitano is saying in regard to her fledgling years with the New York City Opera, "for an opera singer to work in a situation like, for example, the Actors Studio. Frank Corsaro, the opera director, is the only one I know who has a class in acting especially for singers. My dream is to see an 'actors studio' for singers! I would really love that . . . whenever we would be in town we might have a place where we could go and work—not just coaching our voices, which is very important, but also working on our acting. That way, operatic acting wouldn't be such a strange beast. Right now this sort of performing seems to vary from those people who have absolutely no idea what to do with themselves on stage to those who are dramatic virtuosi. I have seen singers with no talent for acting, and they are terribly wooden. But with some good direction they manage to muster up some degree of intensity and theatrical credibility. Admittedly, this is acting of a rather limited form and shape, and it is not the most convincing or the most satisfying for the audience or for fellow artists who are able to do much more with a role.

"I think the current popularity of opera is partially due to the fact that singers have become better actors. Young singers, in particular, are good singer-actors. They are trying to reach a realism in opera that has been inspired not just by the modern theater, but also by the movies and television and even a few of the more remarkable rock performers. You must remember that we were brought up on these things. Not many of us saw the old opera stars who used melodramatic gestures and a type of acting which died in the theater long before it began to vanish from the opera stage. I know for myself . . . I have been very influenced by watching good actors on the screen. And though it is very difficult to translate that kind of naturalistic acting to the operatic stage, there are many of us young singers who are really trying to get closer to that kind of emotional realism. But we really don't have enough opportunity on the working level and study level to evolve these ideas. We have to do it individually by trial and error—or, if we're very lucky, we have a chance to work with the kind of director that the older singers generally loathed: I mean the experimental directors who won't allow you to just stand there on the apron and belt out an aria. These directors are interested in the same new things that interest us as singers."

"Unfortunately," Samuel Ramey says, "that doesn't always work too well. You can end up with a very strange mixture of performances."

"Sam is right. You can see one person on stage performing in this manner while another person is working in an entirely different idiom. More often than not, the way it works out is that there is perhaps one exceptional actor in an opera while everybody else is rather uninspired and wooden. It's possible to cheer the good performer and enjoy what he has achieved, but in the long run his performance really gets in the way of the unity of the production. And that is the biggest problem today in operatic performance. There is no unified acting technique. Directors hardly have the time to block out action, let alone worry—as theater directors do—about unifying the style of the various performers and producing a work with a strong sense of ensemble.

"Opera is still burdened, I think, by generations of singers who thought their egos came first. As a result, we haven't evolved a concept of ensemble acting. We are expected to fight for attention with a baseball bat rather than achieving impact as a group. Sam and I have been exceedingly lucky. We've worked with some really fine directors—not only here in the United States, but also in Europe. This means that we have seen both the possibilities and the problems of working with experimental directors who want us to be more than stereotypes and the older directors who have no interest in anything but stereotypes. It would be nice if everyone were working toward the same goals in opera, but unfortunately they are not."

Samuel Ramey nods in agreement. "I think that dance training of some sort is essential because an opera singer seems to have more in common with the acting done by dancers than people playing realistic characters in a regular play . . . if you see what I mean. Personally, while I was in college, I took a couple of years of dance. It was a class designed for singers and was geared for the kind of awareness of the body which you have to have if you're going to move on stage with any kind of conviction or expressiveness. The opera with a bunch of bodies up there that can't do much of anything is over. I think those days in opera are fast disappearing."

"There is one other thing," Malfitano adds. "Even without training we can still learn something from dance. When we go to a dance performance we're learning something just by watching. And that can sometimes be better than actually taking a class which tries to turn you into a dancer. The problem, as I've already said, is that there is still no place for people who are interested in coordinating all aspects of theater. And I'm not talking on the student level ... I'm talking about a professional coach for opera performers."

"Opera," Ramey interjects, "is a larger-than-life art form. Maybe that's why it reminds us of dancing more than the understated kind of acting that the Actors Studio introduced. Opera is rarely performed in the relatively small theaters where you see plays. And whereas the film actor is seen in huge closeups, the opera performer is generally seen at a very great distance on an immense stage in a huge opera house. It's inevitable that the physical places in which opera is produced will have an impact on the styles we develop in operatic acting. So I think it's only natural that, somewhat like modern dancers and ballet dancers, we use a larger-than-life style."

Catherine Malfitano disagrees: "I'm not certain of that, Sam," she says slowly. "Sometimes I think that I learned a great deal about subtlety from watching film actors. I learned things about small, imaginative gestures and ways of holding myself and walking and leaning ... and things like that. I'm not really so certain that opera requires grand gestures all the time. For instance, I was involved in a new production of *Lucia di Lammermoor* with a young man named David Alden, who is really an excellent director, and we worked toward a kind of naturalness that was much more intimate and not quite so broad and histrionic ... not just big strokes but small, detailed strokes, too. I think that, somehow, when you do a lot of contemporary operas, as I have done, you begin to think differently about acting because the libretti are based on contemporary themes rather than the very idealized characterization of the older operas. For me, the kind of acting I have seen on the screen has always been a better key to what I've attempted as an operatic singer than the performances of the older singers who tended to be very broad and bold about everything. By doing this, young singers are bucking the tradition-bound opera house managements which believe that opera is supposed to be performed in a certain way, and they are afraid of seeing it performed differently. Probably that's the reason why directors like Frank Corsaro are always looked upon as such madmen by conservative people. Naturally he has made some mistakes. But any director who has the desire to see something new and exciting has to take chances, and that sometimes results in peculiar things. For instance, I've been involved in very far-out productions of *Figaro*. The New York City Opera production is not a very daring version of the opera. It's lovely and it's effective, but I've been involved in other productions with directors like Götz Friedrich and Jean-Pierre Ponnelle, and both of them were exceedingly experimental in terms of trying to create characters and trying to answer some of the fundamental questions which the libretto of *The Marriage of Figaro* raises for thinking people. Many people loathed these productions, but I liked them because I think opera shouldn't be so cut and dried and so intent upon being pretty that everything else is forgotten."

"Well, Catherine," Ramey says, "I'm all for invention and daring in opera, but I also think that our production of *Figaro* at the New York City Opera is pretty marvelous. Generally, you know, *Figaro* is produced as if it's just a harmless evening of laughs and doesn't have anything much to say. And that's not what *Figaro* is really about. This production by director John Copley is very fine."

"I couldn't agree more," Catherine says enthusiastically. "A director like Copley, who has a great sense of humor and loves to laugh—he's really a very funny man—well, working with him was wonderful because in rehearsals we didn't stop laughing. So you see, he has a funny streak in him and he likes it to come out in his work. But he was also very much striving for serious elements in this *Figaro* in which you and I star. Like the love between Susanna and Figaro is a real thing and not just a foil for sexual gags. I love the way he has directed me as Susanna."

"And the Count, too," Ramey interrupts. "The Count has a dignity and intensity you simply don't find elsewhere. He's a real person and not just a dirty old man. Oh, certainly, he's after Susanna and he's chased a lot of other women, but he really loves Countess Almaviva and really believes that men have a right to their double standard."

"Yes, Sam, you have a good point there. Susanna too ... she doesn't take her assignment lightly to lure the Count into the garden so he can be caught flirting with her. It's a serious matter to her and she is worried about it. This is one day in the lives of all these people and not simply a routine for getting laughs. These operatic characters have feelings."

"And," Ramey adds, "they are motivated by things that drive all of us. It's simply Mozart's genius to show us both the warm human side of the situation as well as its comic aspects. But for greatness, both the human and the comedic are required. In a way, we're lucky, Catherine, because we became part of the opera world at a time when concepts were changing and the immense popular success of opera in America gave all of us unusual opportunities to reach a larger audience than ever before—especially because of television. It was probably people like Norman Treigle, who was very far ahead of his time, and Maria Callas, who actually set this new trend in motion—partly by showing us that you could do something new with acting in opera, with moving on the stage and with creating a new style of emotion in your singing. But there was something else. I think they also showed the producers that a new style of performance could please the crowds and maybe even bring a whole new audience to opera, like Callas did. The potential of success may have been one of the things—rather than simple daring—that provided experimental directors with the rare opportunity to do new things with opera productions."

"And there is something else that happened," Malfitano interjects. "Though I was originally a bit shocked by what Callas did with her voice, I learned from her recordings that operatic acting is not just a matter of making gestures, but it is also a process of the voice itself. Callas created character just with her voice, and after all, that is also part of acting ability in opera. Callas was one of the singers who could really do that kind of vocal acting. No teacher could or would teach anybody to sing like that. But that's what makes somebody great—the fact that they can use all the traditional as well as some unorthodox techniques and turn it into a marvelous personal style."

For a moment Catherine Malfitano nods her head in concentration. Then she adds, "But to tell you the truth, and I think perhaps Sam feels the same, I don't really idolize people. I know that in the past, young people often idolized certain stars and tried to be like them. But I don't think that young singers are like that anymore. Personally, it's funny but I must admit that I don't find any inspiration in other singers. If someone inspires me, it's usually a magnificent actor. It's been that way all my life—it's been film people and dancers. For instance, seeing a Carla Fracci performance of *Giselle* taught me more about acting in the bel canto roles, like *Lucia* or any of the other operas about strange ladies who go mad, than going to see Joan Sutherland or somebody like that. Sutherland teaches me a lot about the singing of the role—but she adds nothing, frankly, to my understanding of operatic acting. Also I must tell you—though it's not at all expected of an opera singer—that I've learned a lot about communication from some of the people in jazz and rock. I loved Janis Joplin. And what she did with her voice was not terribly unlike what Callas did with hers."

"You know," Ramey concludes as we prepare to leave, "it gets very dreary looking at life as nothing more than an opera singer. And what I think Catherine means when she talks about Janis Joplin is that young people in opera today aren't quite so narrow in their perspective. We have grown up in a larger world than kids in the past who were studying to be in the arts. We're not as exclusive, and maybe that's why we have more to say and want to find more ways to say it."

As we open the tall French doors, the sound of people and traffic on Broadway and Sixty-fifth Street filters into the cool midafternoon atmosphere of our hall of mirrors. Catherine Malfitano slips on her black coat, and Samuel Ramey buttons his jacket against the fall chill. "Well," he says quietly, "I guess we are back in the world of people and problems and rehearsal halls."

"Yes . . ." Catherine replies a bit sadly. "You know, Sam, we are all of us here in the theater because in some way or another it crystallizes living for us. Not that we can't also find it in our lives, but for some reason going onto a stage is sort of a celebration for us. We come together and we celebrate a certain aspect of living which we can't normally reach—or at least not very often. That is what art is for me and that is what opera is. And it's marvelous every now and again when you know that every person in the audience is experiencing something private but something which is also very . . . very communal."

"And," Sam adds, "some people call it opera. Other people in other parts of the world call it ritual."

The French doors close with a snap. From the auditorium comes a cascade of broken notes. "No, no, no . . ." someone is saying, "that's not right . . . we must try it again. We must try it again."

Then, after a moment of silence, the music resumes.

A WALK WITH
ALEXANDRO JODOROWSKY

I had always wanted to meet Alexandro Jodorowsky, ever since seeing his 1971 film *El Topo*. Now I was walking with him in the zoo of New York's Central Park on one of the first days of spring. The animals were coming into their bright new coats, sniffing the air through the bars of their terrible little cages, whie Jodorowsky and I wandered freely in the sunlight. A visceral man in his forties, dressed in funky Mexican peasant attire, he is talking about *El Topo*.

"I have made other films, but only one has found its way into people's hearts."

"Many people were confounded by your imagery," I tell him. "I

Alexandro Jodorowsky in El Topo

know a few people who went back to see the film perhaps five or six times in an effort to fathom it."

"For some people it is difficult, but for me it was very easy," he says with a smile. "I don't understand an apple, but still I eat it."

El Topo was one of the most controversial films of the early seventies. It was denied entry at the Cannes Film Festival because the Mexican government (which chopped forty minutes out of it before permitting it to be shown in Mexico) refused to be represented by "a film of overwhelming heretical blasphemies." But Jodorowsky was undaunted. "I knew that many conservative Mexicans would hate my film. They wanted mariachi bands and Spanish hat dancing! They say that I am crazy, that I'm a terrible liar and a sex maniac. Even if I were all of these things and worse—what does that have to do with my film? I am not a saint. I am an artist."

El Topo is a metaphysical western. It is to the psychological western, which started with *High Noon,* what *Performance* is to the 1930s gangster film. *El Topo* presents a series of the most startling and imaginative images assembled by any filmmaker since perhaps *The Cabinet of Dr. Caligari.* It is the creation—almost the sole creation— of Alexandro Jodorowsky: a primitive man who was born of Russian parents in Iquique, Chile. He was raised in Santiago, where he attended two years of faltering college before dropping out. He has directed well over one hundred plays in Mexico City. "But," he contests, "they are very, very conservative productions—very poor. You understand, it is Mexico that backs my work in the theater, and the government insists that I use its money to make foolish middle-class dramas for a nearly illiterate audience of shopkeepers. They are not terrible productions. For Mexico they are not bad. But I wouldn't want you to see them. They are so primitive and amateurish. It's only in my films that I am able to speak freely. But now even films are made for shopkeepers. There is no more art in film."

I am curious about Jodorowsky's political views. Before I can ask him a question on the subject, he interrupts me: "My art is my politics. My art is my revolution. Nothing else."

Yet he was the creator of a highly political, if obscure, comic strip called *Panic Fables* for an extremist right-wing newspaper in Mexico City, where he lived until the success of *El Topo* brought him to

America. "You do what you must to make a living," he says dolefully.

His only film prior to *El Topo* was a short feature called *Fando and Liz,* which was shown at the international film festival in Acapulco, where it bombed. "There are many things in *Fando and Liz* that resemble Fellini's *Satyricon,*" he says with the open friendliness of a child. "But my film was made a full three years before *Satyricon.*"

Whatever shortcomings exist in Jodorowsky's films made before or after *El Topo* (and he may be a one-film director), there is little question that *El Topo* has remained a curiously attractive and much-discussed creation. Jodorowsky created the music, the costumes, and the scenic designs. He also wrote, directed, and starred in the film, using few professional actors. "I find most of my people on the street. I find them the same way that I find locations. I needed a man without legs and one day he knocked at my door. That's how I found all the people. They simply appeared. The dwarf, for instance, I saw her on the street and I spoke to her. She was still a virgin, and when I padded her belly in the film so she would look pregnant, she cried with joy because she had never imagined herself with child. The other two women in the film also came to me. The first woman, the blonde, appeared at my home one day. She was in terrible condition, having taken drugs in great quantities. She had been put in a hospital for mental illness. As soon as I saw her tragic face, I said: 'I will give you a starring role in my film.' And she believed me. She had no idea who I was and I didn't know her name. She took care of my children for six months. One day she said to me: 'My name is Mara.' Then, shortly after we finished *El Topo,* she went away. I have never seen her again. There was also the other woman, the dark-haired woman. I found her dancing at a go-go club. She didn't work there; she worked as an airline attendant. I said: 'I want to make a film with you.' She just smiled and said, 'Good.' After the film, she also disappeared. I've never seen her again."

For a moment Jodorowsky is silent as he gazes distressfully at the animals in their cages. "I am ashamed to be here in this kingdom of animals. I am ashamed to speak in their silent presence. You see, each movement of an animal is the movement of all animals. And the beast, he knows this. But man, he does not know this. We believe that we are singular and special." Then he laughs for no apparent reason. "I do not remember anything I have done or said. A souvenir is something you have not lived fully. The philosopher said, 'You cannot step into the same stream twice.' Yet there is only one stream. So much for realism. I am not interested in reality. We are always told that we must put more reality into our dreams. But I wish to teach that it is more important for us to put dreams into our reality. That is why we are here today. Where do you take me for a walk? To the zoo. Yes? And this is because we are searching among our dreams for our animal images, for our totems from which all of our dreams originate. It is as if I were to find . . ."

Distant chimes suddenly interrupt his words.

"What were you saying?" I ask.

"I do not know. I will not finish my sentence, because nothing is ever finished. It is wrong to attempt to finish anything." Again Jodorowsky smiles trustingly. Now he gazes at the lions that gaze back at him.

ENCOUNTER WITH
TENNESSEE WILLIAMS

At the Plaza Hotel it is precisely 4:48 p.m. under the palms and electrified candelabra of the sumptuous Palm Court. The year is 1971. Elderly gentlemen with meticulous hairpieces and matrons in hats are having coffee and cakes while thin, rusty music is played by a genteel pianist and a strolling violinist. At the little marble tables and among the green upholstered chairs, a fragile veil of privacy is drawn discreetly over the hushed conversations. Narrow beams of white spotlight fall in dramatic shafts from the luminous pinkness of the high ceiling.

As I sit there waiting, it seems as if the room is a setting for a play.

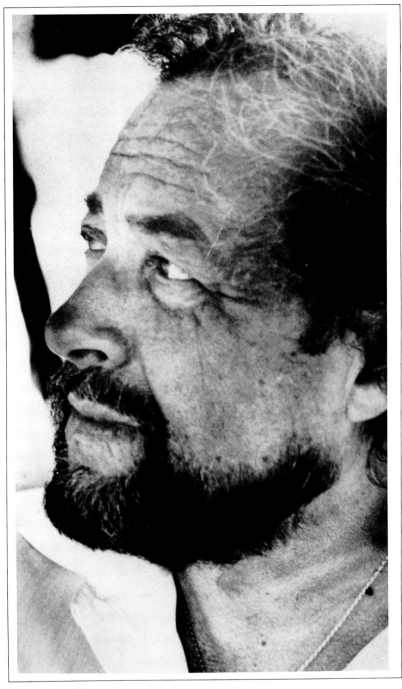

Tennessee Williams

Surely Blanche will make a marvelously melodramatic entrance at any moment, grasping a crushed velvet rose at her breast. Or Laura with a fragile glass animal between her fingers. Stella, Alma, or any of the others in that amazing gallery of slightly grotesque and faded women who populate the dusty worlds of *The Glass Menagerie, A Streetcar Named Desire, Summer and Smoke, The Rose Tattoo, Cat on a Hot Tin Roof, Sweet Bird of Youth,* and *Night of the Iguana.*

Then a little man in a soft white linen suit and panama hat is standing like an aging Puck in the grand entrance of the restaurant. It is Tennessee Williams.

He comes forward. He laughs a bit madly. Then he invites me to accompany him to the dining room despite my hippie garb. The maître d'hôtel unhesitatingly apologizes without as much as glancing at me: "Mr. Williams ... Mr. Williams, I am so terribly sorry, sir," he oozes as if he were advising a gentleman that his dog is not permitted in the restaurant. Williams turns with a controlled abruptness that reeks of indignation and refinement. "I see nothing," he murmurs holding his head aloft, "... absolutely nothing incorrect in the manner in which you are dressed, Mistah Highwaater." And the matter is forgotten as we ascend to his suite.

"I have only the slightest capacity, Mistah Highwaater, to comprehend snobs and mongrels," Tennessee Williams pronounces gracefully as he sits on the edge of his chair and crosses his legs like a boy at his first debutante ball. "I cannot endure rudeness of any kind," he says with the nervous nobility of one of his fading heroines. He smiles without looking at me. I have won him over, it seems, simply by being rejected by a headwaiter. Now he perceives me as one of his favorites: one of the defiant ones. "You are a friend of Mistah James Leo Herlihy I'm told, Mistah Highwaater. Well, gracious, Jamie is a love and I think his writing deserves all of its success! *Midnight Cowboy* made a truly fine film ... truly fine." Then he laughs for no apparent reason as his eyes dart in every direction, anxiously picking up reactions. "My, my, my," he intones, fanning himself with his hand and munching an antacid tablet. "When I can't breathe well," he whispers, "it upsets my stomach. And I just can't for the life of me breathe in New York, Mistah Highwaater. I can't seem to catch my breath!"

A blond, fine-hewn youngster in the manner of an Ingres portrait soundlessly enters and sits rigidly in one of the green chairs at some distance from us. Later the lad is identified as Mr. Williams's private secretary. Immediately after he is seated, a tall, very thin man who looks a bit like a duenna quietly takes his position, also at a distance. They do not speak or look at us. Two waiters wheel in a cart, and the tinkle of ice is deafening in the silence.

Two other gentlemen smile politely as they join us at the coffee table. One looks like an Eton headmaster, while the other looks a bit like one of the apostles.

"And Mistah Lee Hoiby," Williams intones with lavish courtesy, indicating the apostle, "wrote an opera! Yes, an opera based on my play *Summer and Smoke,* which pleases me greatly." I knew and admired Hoiby's music, and eventually we became close friends.

Tennessee Williams smiles as he glances at me. "You and Mistah Hoiby should get on very well indeed, since you are both lovers of great music."

Williams laughs again and looks around the room very graciously. He is a gentle man with a refinement rare among celebrities. There is also something violently suspicious about his manner.

"Plays are only conceived on paper; they are born on the stage," Williams pronounces gravely as if speaking a line out of one of his scripts. "The out-of-town productions are the births. It is never all there, but it will be by the time a play opens. And if you are lucky enough to get through the out-of-town critics, then, of course, you go on to New York!"

I ask if he is still an enthusiast of playwright Edward Albee.

"I liked his play *All Over,*" he leans toward me and confides. "It got, perhaps, a little pompous at points, but the overall effect was stunning, simply stunning. Very pure . . . yes, very pure indeed. He's so uncompromising, this Edward Albee, he's so pure. Do you happen to know him?"

I say that I do.

"My goodness, then I must watch what I say," Williams laughs with a trace of sarcasm. "I don't think that your friend Mr. Albee ever thinks about reaction. No more than Beckett or Ionesco. I always want to please," he says perplexedly, as if he were thinking aloud. "That's why I'm an inferior artist, because I always want to please. If I had written a play like *All Over,* you know, Mistah High-waaater, I would have been very upset about the press notices. But they had a serious audience the night I was there. *Everyone* listened! Spellbound! But if I had written *All Over,* believe me, it would have closed in a week. Because, you see, I don't have an audience. I had one but I lost it. I lost it back in the midsixties ... yes, I'm quite aware of that, sir. I lost my audience."

"But isn't it true," I offer with compulsive compassion, "that Albee, too, has lost his audience? And don't all great creators go through an awkward period in which they are abandoned before they are rediscovered?"

He ignores my comment. "My new plays," he says with a sour smile, "do not get the kind of attention that *All Over* got even though it was considered a flop. There is the difference."

"But," I insist, "your plays are finding a whole new audience among young people. And the films which were made of your plays are some of the best products of the American cinema."

"But, Mistah Highwaaater, my new plays ... well, even my agent doesn't like my new plays. They are, shall we say, too internalized and too difficult."

"What's difficult about them?"

"They are very very personal, for one thing," he confides with a wink, leaning over and whispering to me. "They are about *collapse.*" The word dries in his throat. He is unquestionably referring to his confinement in a mental hospital from which he had only recently been released. "And ... it's difficult to say what these new plays are really about. But I'll tell you this: they affirm nothing ... but gallantry in the face of defeat." Then, unexpectedly, he giggles.

"Isn't it rather curious," I suggest, "that though you feel somewhat uncomfortable among actors and, as Jamie Herlihy told me, you have few actors as friends, still you've written plays about them?"

"Oh, my land," he retorts. "I've written often about actors! Yes, indeed. My dear mother says, 'For God's sake, Tom, never write another thing about an aging actress! It'll be the death of you!' "

Everyone laughs politely except the blond boy, who sits as remote from us as a character in an Antonioni film.

"A two-character play of mine is about an aging actress and her brother. This was a play," he says painfully, "which I wrote in the late sixties when I was mentally broken. I rewrote it after my release from . . . the hospital. After I managed to con my way out of the boobie hatch where my brother put me."

Now Tennessee Williams is not laughing. He looks at me with an almost resentful stare for a moment . . . as if my very presence were forcing this unrelenting candor from his lips. "I have always been mad, you know, Mistah Highwaater. Always. That is the natural state of the artist. From the brink of madness this play should have illuminated what I have been trying to say during my whole career. It could have . . . but it didn't. One is not as young at sixty as one is at thirty. I have to rewrite and rewrite and rewrite now. Not that you don't have a great deal more to say when you are older . . . because, of course, you do. If I could only have written this play with the vigor that I had when I wrote *Menagerie* . . . then this would surely have been my greatest play." And he smiles thinly and pauses for a moment. Then he says very flatly: "Unfortunately, it wasn't."

He nods with exhaustion and glances away for a moment. "You know," he says, turning slowly to look me hard in the eye, "writing is a physical activity . . . like dancing. But even more physically difficult. When you are reaching . . . reaching for those ultimate words and images, it's like the most intense kind of work! I actually pant for breath when I'm reaching for that kind of *real* inspiration!" As he speaks, his eyes blaze momentarily, and I recall Blanche in *A Streetcar Named Desire,* who gasps for breath, on the verge of suffocation.

Then Tennessee Williams sinks silently into himself. I can see in his face something of the same calamity that makes Blanche cry out against barbarism and coarseness. He smiles at me weakly, as if he has understood my thoughts. And then the avalanche of fear tumbles back into his features. It is like Blanche—pressed against the wall with her flashing Vivien Leigh eyes, dashing to the table and panting into the telephone: "Fire! Fire!" For Tennessee Williams it may be a call for help from the same fire in which both genius and madness burn recklessly. "Fire! Fire!"

DISCOVERING
LUCIA DLUGOSZEWSKI

There is a verse by the Japanese poet Basho that resounds of my long friendship with Lucia Dlugoszewski:

> The voice of the bell
> As it leaves the bell!

It was through Lucia that I came to know R. H. Blyth's translations of haikus. It was through her that I met F. S. C. Northrop, whose writings had already made a profound impact on me. And because of Lucia I came to know Robert Motherwell, Isamu No-

Lucia Dlugoszewski

guchi, Djuna Barnes, Joseph Campbell, Lillian Kiesler, and Virgil Thomson.

Lucia Dlugoszewski came to New York from Detroit in the 1940's to study piano with Grete Sultan and composition with Felix Salzer and Edgard Varèse. She arrived in Manhattan when she was still very young. But she was terribly bright, entirely liberated, and exceptionally articulate, and soon the artistic leaders of the era came to adore her. And what an era it was! Those were the great days of abstract expressionism. Frank O'Hara gave Lucia New York. There was hardly a major innovator in the arts who did not somehow touch her life and whose life was not touched by her. She wears that unique initiation into the many worlds of art like a cloak of dreams . . . *the voice of the bell.*

I have known Lucia since the days when I was a very young man in San Francisco. She was rehearsing her full-evening score on timbre piano for *Here and Now with Watchers* in our auditorium in the late fifties, and I sat in the darkness in the last row and listened for hour upon hour, utterly fascinated by her music.

We became friends almost as soon as we met, captivated by hearing our ideas articulated by another human being. But these were not simply "ideas." They were passions that we lived every day of our lives. Those lives have become very complex since those innocent days. Through it all, our friendship has persisted because we share an obsession with a vision of the world of the arts as a place of *living* people . . . not merely of celebrities or personalities, but members of a community of thinkers and creators who keep the world alive for us.

During the thirty years that I have known Lucia, she has insistently given her creative energies to other people, even to such an extent that—to my annoyance—she has sometimes neglected her own talents. It is especially significant, therefore, that despite such self-neglect she has won very considerable praise from her peers. Most recently she was awarded the Koussevitzky International Record Award for the recording of her "Fire Fragile Flight."

I have so often listened to Lucia Dlugoszewski sing the praises of other artists that I have decided to devote a few lines of praise to her unique art. Her music doesn't fit easily into any category of contemporary composition. The language and intellect that characterize Lucia and are imbued in her music are highly rarified. Yet, paradoxically, performances of her works inevitably produce intense feeling and sensual clarity. It is this contrast of complex rationality and total immediacy that distinguishes both the inventiveness of her music and the primal heritage from which it springs. For, ultimately, Lucia Dlugoszewski's music is both ultramodern and very ancient.

Fluidity and contrast are probably the most characteristic elements of her scores. The music is not simply a denial of the rigidity and linear sense of form and development of classicism, nor is it a retreat into the emotionalism that often marks works of the Romantic tradition. Dlugoszewski composes music filled with expression but unmarked by emotion. Through complexity of structure her works provide a sense of directness, flow, and freedom. The music is often massive in its layers of sound, and the sense of sonic invention is undoubtedly remarkable, yet neither craft nor novelty are in any way central to the impact of her style. The cumulative effect, as with the music of most remarkable composers, is of music that is both unique and familiar.

These descriptions of sound that bounds outward and upward in every direction, of great clusters and layers of tone, shouldn't suggest that Dlugoszewski lacks a capacity for lyricism. Some of her most expressive works are filled with episodes of unequalled delicacy and vulnerability. In fact it is vulnerability as a human condition that is the most persistent and moving theme in her music. Yet, even in such deeply felt moments, there is no hint of pictorial emotion, operatic gesture, or sentimentality.

We can credit Dlugoszewski, as Virgil Thomson has done, with strikingly ingenious instrumental virtuosities and sonic originality, but we must not do so at the expense of something more fundamental in her music: its unmatched poetic shape and impact, which, like metaphor in language, breaks out of its own restrictions and—with vast imaginal inference and resonance—expresses for us things yet unknown.

WATCHING
ROBERT MOTHERWELL

Robert Motherwell reminds us that the body is an organ of perception. He suggests that art is a form of transformation. He confirms that "seeing" is not simply an activity of the eye.

These metaphysical conceits were my overwhelming response to an exhibition of the art of Motherwell at the William Benton Museum of the University of Connecticut at Storrs. Entitled Robert Motherwell and Black and comprising ninety pieces handsomely installed to fill the museum to capacity, the show is dominated by works in black and champions the artist's conception of black as a color and not simply a tone or buffer for other hues. Among the

Robert Motherwell

works on canvas were paintings like *The Spanish Death, In Plato's Cave No. 1,* and *In Black and White No. 2.* Pieces from such illustrious Motherwell series as *Iberia, Je t'aime,* and *Lyric Suite,* as well as some of the artist's most exceptional prints (with selections from the Livre d'artiste, *A la pintura,* of 1972) were among the rhythmical succession of images. Though the exhibition subtly dealt with the metaphor of black as a color, another side of Motherwell was much in evidence: his stunning and essential use of color. Three of his most revelational color explorations could be seen in the large collage of six red components entitled *Voluptuousness with Bar Sinister* (1976), as well as in *Phoenician Red* (1977) and the eloquent *Red Sea* (1976). Yet even in these dazzling invocations of color, the magnetic impact of black remained a central force in Motherwell's uncommonly brilliant art.

What radiated from the cumulative experience of this landmark exhibition was the image of Motherwell himself—a stately man of firm conviction as well as immense humanity, an artist of great refinement and intelligence. Everywhere in his work is an animation and keenness that matches his personal magnitude. But don't think for a moment that I am promoting the romantic contention that smart people don't make great artists or the cliché that Motherwell is an "intellectual painter who talks a good painting." Quite to the contrary, he achieves an expression that utterly outdistances intellect. He has succeeded again and again in expressing the most evolved, informed, and articulate sensibility in purely painterly terms. What makes Motherwell unique both as a person and as an artist is his capacity to deny his intellect and, in so doing, to conduct us more deeply than any other living American painter into the imagination. This capacity to illuminate a visionary realm is surely a result of Motherwell's exceptional intelligence, but behind his articulate cerebration is the marvelous nakedness of the paintings themselves.

In some ways, Motherwell embodies the Eastern idea of using one's ability as a thinker to reach a place where thought cannot penetrate.

I recall the evening in 1980 when I met Robert Motherwell. He had just presented an award of merit to Erick Hawkins on behalf of

Dance Magazine. "In your book on dance," he said to me while we toasted the occasion, "you bring up some ideas with which I very much agree. You say that dancers don't dance with their bodies. You say that they have to give up their bodies in order to achieve a dance."

I nodded in agreement.

"But do you know that painters must do something very similar. They must give their bodies to their painting. Their bodies become the painting."

This notion of transformation is fundamental to Motherwell's thinking, and he came to it through a succession of encounters with the French symbolists and surrealists. This French influence, however, did not require the kind of Parisian sojourn that greatly influenced American artists of the twenties, such as Virgil Thomson, Gertrude Stein, and other renowned members of the Lost Generation. Motherwell's experience with French aesthetics took place in wartime New York.

Today Motherwell resides in Greenwich, Connecticut. He was born in Aberdeen, Washington, in 1915 and spent his formative years in California. He came east to attend Harvard in 1937, where he majored in philosophy. Through the influence of the great art historian Meyer Schapiro, Motherwell eventually abandoned his classical and philosophical program of study and decided to devote himself to painting. Through Schapiro, the young Motherwell met the French surrealist writers and painters who became refugees in New York after the fall of Paris to the Nazis. His classical education blended with the avant-garde ideologies of the French symbolist poets and the emerging insights of psychoanalysis. The result was unique; Motherwell rejected the surrealists' approach to picture making at the same time that he embraced their theory of automatism—a process of relinquishing consciousness during the creative act and relying, instead, upon a more intuitional mentality. As such, there is in the works of Robert Motherwell a rationale entirely original and a mentality that evokes the words of anthropologist Lucien Lévy-Bruhl: ". . . the reality in which [primal and tribal] peoples move is itself mystical." That reality is very familiar to Motherwell.

It is implicit in his close ties to contemporary French aesthetics. It was Paul Valéry who said that the painter "takes his body with him." Another Frenchman, phenomenologist Maurice Merleau-Ponty added to this conviction when he said: "It is by lending his body to the world that the artist changes the world into paintings."

These statements are clearly metaphors for the kind of transformational experience discovered in the works of Robert Motherwell, metaphors to which he alluded when he told me that the body of the painter "becomes the painting."

Motherwell's images are not puzzling signs that obscurely substitute for common-sense reality. They are not distortions or abstractions that allude to hidden meanings. Motherwell's paintings mean what they are. And to share that meaning we must become the painting we are seeing, for that is the creative aspect of any visionary activity. Just as Motherwell is necessarily transformed into what he paints by the very process of making images, so we must allow ourselves to become part of the painting in order to experience it. We cannot expect anything to happen to us when we simply *look* at or try to *understand* a work of art. It is little wonder that people who expect to experience art by merely looking and understanding are constantly frustrated and infuriated by their failure to respond to what is in front of them. A diagram may be a realistic statement about life. But it is not life. A diagram is a blueprint, a substitute for life. And that's very easy. A painting is life itself. And that is not easy.

For Robert Motherwell, art is an effervescence of living, or as Merleau-Ponty observed, "it is impossible to say that nature ends there and that man or expression starts here."

The work of Robert Motherwell is a testament to an alternative perception of the world. Of all the so-called abstract expressionists, Motherwell (the youngest of the founders) has a unique and powerful capacity for combining expression and color. What he has achieved is an elaborate array of visual conventions built upon an entirely different conception of "seeing" from the one previously understood in Western culture. This imagery springs from the innermost consciousness of the artist, and in learning to grasp its aesthetic premises, we managed to slip past ourselves and the stern sentries of our cultural isolation. We peer momentarily into a reflection of ourselves from the other side of perception. Robert Motherwell opens up the real with the imagery of the abstract, giving us a brief look inside before the door slams shut. Without art, that door remains forever closed. Without art we are alone.

MUSIC NEEDS MORE RAINBOWS

There is something that bothers me about the musical traditions of the West. I have always felt just a bit uncomfortable with the performing mannerisms of classical music: its tux-clad or black-draped musicians, its folding chairs and bleak lights on stage, and the program-clutching, stiffly regimented audience, self-consciously *not* applauding between movements, but confusedly clapping between the segments of a song cycle, shouting the bravo/brava/bravi borrowed from Italy but never shouting out a good old Ivesian Hooray! as they might at an exciting sport event. We seem to be a culture without an indigenous and genuine ceremony for our musical theater, not on the stage and not in the audience. It seems very sad to me that we have produced so little ritual and so much etiquette.

Two groups of performers at Carnegie Hall helped me to focus on these feelings: the soloists of the Ensemble Nipponia and the Boston Symphony conducted by Seiji Ozawa in a program that included George Crumb's *Echoes of Time and the River: Four Processionals for Orchestra.*

The program of the Ensemble Nipponia consisted of four works in the traditional form and a transitional composition by Katsutoshi Nagasawa demonstrating the effort in Japan at the turn of the century and thereafter to assimilate the musical ideals of the West while still employing traditional instruments. The Nagasawa piece was followed by three contemporary works by Minoru Miki, artistic director of the Ensemble Nipponia and a well-known composer in Japan, though not a celebrity in America like Toru Takemitsu and Toshiro Mayuzumi. From the outset of the program there was a fundamental quality and character totally alien in the Western concert hall. Immediate silence was prompted by the appearance of a single gliding musician, Kohachiro Miyata, as he delicately moved across the stage, ceremonially holding his recorderlike instrument (called a shakuhachi) and pausing to remove his slippers before ascending to the special platform provided for the musicians. There he turned to the audience, bowed once officiously, and knelt in one perfect movement, and with a precision no less marvelous than that with which he eventually performed, he lifted his beautifully crafted instrument and placed it with the elegance of a dancer to his lips.

My point is this: even before he had begun to play, a ritual implicit to his music had already been performed. Every gesture and every element of the first half of the program was of the same spirit: the screens behind the musicians, the red-clad platform, the regal costumes and headdresses, the elaborately crafted instruments, and even the vast and lush tangle of branches, flowers, and bark that adorned the stage at Carnegie Hall.

With the music of Nagasawa and Miki the atmosphere changed abruptly: the conventional folding chairs appeared on stage along with a modern, twenty-string koto developed in 1969 and standing (keyboard height) on a modern podium. The ideals of the West enriched Japanese music, but also brought the decline of the ritual that had been integral to the Asian performing arts for a thousand years. The music of Minoru Miki was fascinating and highly inventive, but the performance lost something that postwar Japan also lost: cultural integrity.

The victors of the Western world, as we all know, have won everything, and in the process they have lost themselves. This loss is very deeply felt by various cults and clans that continually borrow from other cultures. The loss of an ethos in the West is also felt by many artists who attempt to create rites of their own to fill the void left by a lack of rituals integral to their societies. James Joyce, Carl Jung, Franz Kafka, Karlheinz Stockhausen, Robert Motherwell, Gabriel García Márquez, Robert Wilson, Pablo Picasso, Federico García Lorca, Erick Hawkins, Arthur Rimbaud, and Meredith Monk are a small part of the extensive list of artists who built a *mysterious self* through their art in order to fill the vacuum left by the lack of a public ceremonial life.

Is it any wonder that a composer such as George Crumb should attempt to regrasp the nature of music as a ritual act and that conductor Ozawa and his Boston musicians should attempt, perhaps very self-consciously and awkwardly, to realize Crumb's difficult but wonderful purpose? I don't think so.

Crumb is such a wise producer of theatrical music that I tend to be suspicious of my enthusiasm for his very great achievements in a work like *Echoes of Time and the River.* One hearing in a thoroughly hostile audience was not sufficient exposure to form a judgment, but on the basis of that one performance I feel certain ideas very strongly.

The four processionals for orchestra are exactly that: brilliantly conceived actions by the musicians themselves. Much of the sonic newness of the piece was anticipated by innovations by other composers (Berg, Stockhausen, Berio, et al.): whistling, whispering, and declamations by the musicians. Bartók had previously envisioned a "stereo" effect in the concert hall achieved by the placement of instrumentalists, and several contemporary composers have experimented with musicians moving around the stage during the performance. Nothing, however, has synthesized these experiments into a consummate ritual-work as handsomely, effectively, and musically as Crumb's *Echoes of Time and the River*. From the outset, when three musicians move across the stage while playing their own ritual music, it becomes evident how exceptionally beautiful Western instruments are and how rarely we really see them. It becomes evident how perfectly the traditional black "costumes" of musicians serve to offset the contours, glint, and complex sculpture of the musical implements they carry. The musicians' staccato whisper, "Montani semper liberei," as they cross the stage is a mysterious event—utterly riveting in its subtlety. Then, in the second processional, in single file black-clad men slowly move to the very edge of the stage and stand there momentarily, facing us. Then they lift their trumpets, French horns, and trombones (what glistening, exotic objects they suddenly become!) and blow through these instruments. But no "music" is heard—only the wailing of breath itself—a preface for a fragment from Spanish poet García Lorca that is whispered into the trombones: "Los Acros rotos donde sufre el tiempo." No blast of trumpets, but something so utterly fundamental that we are astonished to hear it. And what we hear from this imposing line of shining instruments is the *breath* that is life itself to music. It is like seeing a great actor stride to the very brink of the stage and open her mouth to voice something so deeply felt, so primal that it is neither word nor outcry, neither sigh nor symbol—but the ineffable *thing* itself: that which precedes speech and thought, that which is the raw experience itself structured into an event—that which we call *ritual*.

And what, after all, is this mysterious event that has eluded the Western world? Long ago I found the answer to that question in the essays of Suzanne Langer. It is an appearance . . . an apparition, if you like. It springs from what we do, but it is not what we are. It is something else. A shadow. The light that we have within us, casting a shadow at once alien and familiar.

In watching a ritual, we do not experience what is physically before us. What we see is an interaction of forces by which something else arises. Those who only *look* at what is before them are incapable of *seeing*. Ritual requires us to see. To see a virtual image that is not unreal, for when we are confronted by it, it really does exist, but which is unsubstantial like a shadow. The reflection in a mirror is such an image . . . and so too is a rainbow. The rainbow seems to stand on earth and in the clouds, but it really "stands" nowhere. It is only visible, not tangible. It is the ultimate fiction: the unspeakable, the ineffable made visible, made experiential.

That Western musicians are not trained in movement as Japanese musicians are, that they are never or rarely part of a larger, theatrical (ritual) experience, unless they are shut off from it in the pit, makes them poorly prepared to undertake what George Crumb and Seiji Ozawa asked of them at Carnegie Hall. Much of the downstairs audience seemed to feel duped by the performance. The man behind me was so outraged that he demanded to know why I was applauding. "It's people like you who encourage this kind of crap!" he shouted at me.

The response only shows how far some of us have come from the real world, which technology is determined to subdue and to conquer. Some people only want realism! They want things that they can reach out and touch! They want musical athletes—virtuosi. They want real music that they can hum. They want to be uplifted by rockets and supersonic aircraft in the theater and in the concert hall. They want to be taken somewhere over the rainbow, no doubt. But what they need and what music needs is more rainbows.

CONVERSATION WITH
JOSEPH CAMPBELL

This unassuming Greenwich Village restaurant is one of Joseph Campbell's favorite haunts. He sits over a scotch in the deserted little dining room, waiting for a hefty order of manicotti all'etrusca. The Italian restaurateur and his three waiters chatter, scurry, and generally fuss over this great man, whose books they have not read but whose intellectual charisma is instantly apparent to them.

"Quiet . . . quiet," the owner whispers to the young man who is nervously serving my spaghetti. "You must not interrupt such a serious conversation!"

The owner of the restaurant does not know me, but my prestige

Joseph Campbell

has been remarkably increased because I am dining with Campbell.

I first met Joseph Campbell when he invited me to Big Sur in the early 1980s to participate in the filming of a television series devoted to his acclaimed studies in world mythology. On the first day of filming at Big Sur, Campbell and I found ourselves in the company of a remarkably prosaic person—a renowned Nobel laureate in biology who insisted that "a myth is something that is untrue." For Joseph Campbell such a statement was clearly absurd. I recall the expression of dismay that filled his face as he gazed at the biologist and said: "Things don't have to be true to be meaningful. Our problem in the West is that we are always trying to find a concrete basis for our beliefs. We always want to turn poetry into prose."

Our biologist friend, however, was not impressed with Campbell's argument.

"Something is either true or it is not true," the laureate insisted.

Suddenly Campbell's demonic side caught fire, and with a subtle grin he said, "You know, my friend, the biggest trouble with Jehovah is that he thinks he's God!"

The delighted look of recognition that passed between Campbell and me became the basis of our friendship.

The Italian waiters clear the table and bring out a full bottle of liquor and black coffee. Joseph Campbell sips slowly and smiles with undisguised pleasure.

"I was always interested in the work I'm doing now," he says. "I spent much of my childhood roaming among the Indian relics at the American Museum of Natural History. The stuff just fascinated me! Then when I was no more than five years old, the Buffalo Bill Wild West Show came to New York . . . with a whole bunch of Indians right off the plains!" he exclaims. "And then, at prep school, a whole splash of books about the south seas started coming out. One of them had immense impact on me. It was by Frederick O'Brian and called *White Shadows in the South Seas*. And all that ethnic material really got to me! I was brought up a Catholic, you know, and it didn't take me very long to see the connections between my religion and a lot of the same motifs in other mythologies. And when I finally discovered those wonderful Arthurian legends as a college student, I saw all the same motifs coming up again: resurrection and rebirth, religious ordeals and divination. Those universalities of myth are the things I hope we got into the film we made in California."

During a break in the filming at Big Sur, as a result of one of the greatest storms in local history, I came to know a good deal about the events and circumstances that produced Joseph Campbell. He was born in New York City in 1904—a date I find almost impossible to comprehend, given the sharpness of mind, apparent physical youth, and intellectual adventurousness of this one-time track and field athlete, who was educated at Columbia University.

He also did some postgraduate work in Europe. "It was in Paris and Munich, while taking some courses, that I first encountered the works of people like James Joyce, Thomas Mann, and Carl Jung; and I also came face to face with the whole phenomenon of modern art and its relationship to myth—especially among the surrealists, who were very active at the time. Then I came back to New York in 1929. Two weeks later Wall Street crashed! That brought my formal education to an abrupt end. My family had no funds, and I found myself out of work. So I left college, not only because I was out of money but also because I was disenchanted with formal education. I had learned so much in Europe that I didn't want to continue work on a thesis I had previously started at Columbia University. And my adviser wouldn't let me change my approach or the subject I was writing about. So I just said to hell with it.

"I lived in Woodstock for five years in a little shack that cost twenty dollars a year. I wasn't yet married, and so I managed to stick it out, spending all my time reading everything that was essential to the kind of thinking I was doing in those days. I had an old Model T Ford, and I decided to drive out to California, looking for work along the way. But there weren't any jobs, and I ended up in Carmel, on the California coast. That's where I spent a couple of months with John Steinbeck and his collaborator, biologist Ed Rickets. It was Ed who was especially important to me, because he reinforced the interest in biology that I had had as a prep-school student. And from our long talks about biology, I eventually came up with one of my basic viewpoints: that myth is a function of biology. It's a manifestation of the human imagination which is stirred by the energies of the organs of the body operating against one another. In other words, myth is as fundamental to us as our capacity to speak and think and dream."

Eventually Campbell came back to New York and settled into a faculty position at Sarah Lawrence College, where he remained rather quietly for thirty-eight years. This reclusiveness was not intentional. To the contrary, Campbell is a highly public and gregarious man with a splendid wit and a finely wrought sense of the world. He clearly understands that what he has written and what he has to say are important. He gradually developed a reputation with a special audience. For most of the public, however, Campbell did not exist until a couple of years ago, when Bill Moyers devoted two exceptional PBS programs to Campbell's life and works.

"Everybody seems to think that Moyers gave birth to me," the eighty-year-old mythologist quips as a bright smile fills his youthful face. "The people who discovered my work through those television interviews don't often realize that I had spent years writing books and lecturing!"

Joseph Campbell's unique viewpoint was not always regarded with high esteem by publishers. He tells an amusing story about his first book. "I started writing on the things I used to say to my students at Sarah Lawrence. I finished off a huge stack of pages, cut it up, and called the first part *The Hero with a Thousand Faces.* I wrapped it up and sent it off without an agent, directly to a publisher. Then there was a very long silence. When I asked about the manuscript, I was told there was no interest in the subject."

Later Kurt Wolf at Pantheon declined it with the glib remark, "Who the hell will read it?"

As a last resort, Campbell sent the book to the Bollingen Foundation, which publishes through Princeton University Press. "After a few weeks I got a telegram from them saying, 'The Hero is a honey.' It's been a big seller for Bollingen—and that's how my career as a writer began."

I quote from the American artist Arthur Dove, and Campbell nods his appreciation of the words: "Dove said that we cannot express the light in nature because we have not the sun. He said that we can only express the light we have in ourselves."

"Exactly!" Campbell exclaims. "Myths are our means of expressing the light within us!" In our lives, he explains, we try every
means of escaping the ordinary. Even the most mundane people de-
spise being prosaic, and when we recount the simplest story it becomes something else: we embellish and extend reality into a "tall
tale." Such tall tales are simply the most common result of a profound human disposition: the making of myths that externalize an
interior reality that is truer than the reality before us.

Joseph Campbell tells us that "it is a curious characteristic of our
unformed species that we live and model our lives through acts of
make-believe." We are myth makers. We are legenders. Of all the animals we alone are capable of dreaming ourselves into existence.

That is Joseph Campbell's central concept.

Campbell tells us that the first function of a mythology is to
waken and maintain in the individual a sense of wonder and partici-
pation in the mystery of this finally inscrutable cosmos. "Mythologies differ as the horizons, landscapes, sciences, and technologies of
their civilizations differ," he explains. The essential function of
mythologies is the instruction of the group and the individual in
"the passages of human life, from the stage of dependency in childhood to the responsibilities of maturity, and on to old age and the
ultimate passage of the dark gate."

Such poetic language is typical of Campbell, for he clearly understands the need to make his ideas significant to readers and listeners.

"Calling people like me popularizers is an evasion of a serious
conflict in our society. This is also the dilemma of the English writer
C. P. Snow. He talks about the 'two cultures' we live in: the hu-
manist's culture on the one hand and then the scientist's culture on
the other. These different world views are growing farther and farther apart. In our society we've reached the point where we attempt
to understand *everything* in terms of technology, and we greatly ne-
glect the humanistic interpretation. What this means is that we approach the world only for its factual content and totally disregard its
expressive, human meanings. In mythology and art, particularly,
these two views—humanism and scientism—simply *have* to be
brought together. Art and myth can't work any other way. And
writers who are not interested in both sides of the subject are failing

to deal with the whole range of implications that are really at the core of both myth and art. We need both the scientific research that determines the facts and the evaluation of those facts in humanistic terms. You see, this human element is essential because myth and art are the souls of a people. And you're really not talking about a culture and its people until you are able to grasp the human expressiveness intrinsic to myth and art.

"It's the artist who really finds the images that are poetic, human, and universal. And that's what a mythology is all about: it's poetry rather than prose. Art and myth are metaphors simply because they must deal with the ineffable, and the only way human beings can do that is through the use of symbols and poetic images that express things that are otherwise unspeakable."

Is Campbell saying that the world of the psyche is more important than the social world?

"No," he explains. "A lot of writers after the time of Freud concentrated so much upon the 'psychological' meaning of art that art ceased to have any social dimension. On the other hand, people in science took no notice of anything but observable data—which also fails to grasp the wholeness of human experience. My own work assumes that there is such a thing as a human species with a human psyche, and therefore I definitely believe that we can understand something about various cultures that seem to be out of our reach—because they no longer exist or because they are exceptionally different from us. Naturally there is immense diversity in the way we manifest our basic human qualities, and there will always be great differences between one culture and another. But that does not deny the fact that we are all human and we all possess the same minds and spirits. Certain ideas are constant in every culture: the promised land, virgin birth, resurrection, the notion of an afterlife, an initiation into adulthood . . . all of these things are common factors of the human psyche. But then we must also recognize the *ethnic* ideas, which are the local interpretations of these universal messages from our psyches. And that's when you get cultural diversity.

"Without a sense of the universality of the human mind, we tend to turn everything we encounter that's different from ourselves into a *curiosity*. To look at any art without a sense of poetry, without a capacity for metaphor, leaves us with nothing but dead objects which decorate our walls. In the West, we've stressed the vulgar interpretation rather than the poetic image, having mistaken the metaphor for the message, having confused the menu with the meal, and now we're left munching, as it were, on cardboard."

Then is there something artificial about the current interest in the ethnic arts of Africa, Oceania, and Indian America? Do visitors to museums have the slightest hope of having any sort of significant response to art that is produced by an entirely alien ethnicity?

"The African mask in a museum poses problems because most of us are unfamiliar with the social and mythological significance of that object in terms of its own culture. Yet there is such a thing as an aesthetic experience. It's the means by which we can enter into a completely alien experience. But how far an artistic response can take us toward 'understanding' an alien work of art depends on how much we actually know about the society that produced the art. Obviously the ideal approach to so-called ethnic art should combine knowledge and information with aesthetic sensitivity. But information alone is not enough, and many of us have been taught to believe that information is all there is to 'art appreciation.' Viewers have to possess something of the artist in themselves if they are going to experience the achievements of art. That aesthetic capacity is in all of us. It's part of our heritage as human beings. But not all of us are in touch with it."

Ezra Pound, in 1937, wrote that "it has taken us two thousand years to get round again to meditating on mythology." Almost fifty years later, this remark is still powerfully suggestive. As Herbert L. Schneidau has said: "It may be that the most important development of twentieth-century consciousness has to do not with atom bombs or moon walks, but with a new seriousness toward prehistory and mythology."

Campbell has reminded us that we do not have the sun, and yet we must have a light so we can find our way through the unspeakable darkness of our inscrutable cosmos. The imagination illuminates and, finally, defines our *only* reality—the only truth we can know. That light is a mythic lantern. And the world that it illuminates for us is the realm of rituals by which we know ourselves and what we have been and what we are becoming.

"We can only express the light we have within us," Campbell reaffirms as we shake hands on the windy corner of Sixth Avenue and Waverly Place.

Campbell gazes down the cluttered street while litter tumbles in the swift breeze and a procession of spectacularly peculiar Village people staggers around us. "I'm very excited about the second volume of my new *Historical Atlas of World Mythology*," he exclaims with an energetic gesture of his hands. "Just wait till you read it! It's one of the best things I've ever done!"

I watch him as he saunters across the street, agile and brisk, strangely unaffected by the city's delirium. He turns toward me with a final wave of his arm, exclaiming: "Don't forget: what counts is the light we have within us!"

And then he is gone.

CODA:
DEAR MR. SALIERI

We can easily reduce our detractors to absurdity and show
them their hostility is groundless. But what does this prove?
Only that their hatred is *real*. When every slander has been
rebutted, every misconception cleared up, every false opinion
about us overcome, intolerance itself will remain finally
irrefutable.

—Moritz Goldstein,
"Deutsch-jüdischer Parnass"

I have been fortunate in living a life filled with exceptional people. I
have also known people who are tormented by their own insignifi-

cance and who detest those who exceed them. And though I would like to believe otherwise, I must admit that we are as much shaped by those who loathe us as by those who love us.

George F. Will has written brilliantly about the "indignation industry"—a mechanism invented for the large population that luxuriates in feeling outraged. He notes that the kind of remarkably gifted people I have celebrated in this book may eventually withdraw from public life or practice extreme self-censorship "lest any thought give some hair-trigger group a pretext for the fun of waxing outraged."

The imagination and its achievements are hateful to people whose unimaginative lives are haunted by failure. As Woody Allen contends, for them "gossip is the new pornography." And the greatest show on earth continues to be an arena where we raise people to incredible heights so we may have the pleasure of watching them tumble to the ground.

Charles Ruas asked Truman Capote if people's attitude toward celebrity has always been like that—"the cannibalizing of the artist the moment a person reaches a certain stature."

Capote said: "They do it to everybody in this country. They do it to film stars; they do it to writers; they do it to painters; they do it to composers. They'll build somebody up and then totally destroy him. I think the toughest thing in the world is to survive decades of creative works, working creatively and consistently, trying to do what you want to do and still survive."

Wherever he is now, Mr. Capote can take heart. We remember Salieri only because of an embattled composer named Mozart.

The music plays on!

ACKNOWLEDGMENTS

Grateful acknowledgment is made to the following for permission to print material copyrighted or controlled by them:

AP/Wide World Photos for the photograph of Linda Eastman.

Artservices for the photograph of Robert Ashley in "Interview with Alvin Lucier" from *Music with Roots in the Aether.* Photo © Philip Makanna.

Columbia Artists Management Inc. for the photograph of Catherine Malfitano. Photo: Stan Fellerman.

Anna Halprin for the photograph of herself in *The Prophetess.*

James Leo Herlihy for the photograph of himself, "Jamie, 1982," and the painting "Portrait of Anaïs Nin" by Claude Michel Seren.

M. Knoedler & Co., Inc., for the photograph of Robert Motherwell. Photo: Renate Ponsold, copyright © 1983.

Richard Kostelanetz for the photograph of himself by J. Nebraska Gifford.

David B. LaClaire for the photograph of Joseph Campbell, copyright © David B. LaClaire, 1983, Grand Rapids, Michigan.

Chic Lloyd for the photograph of Robin Wagner and Jamake Highwater.

Lee Marshall for the photograph of Janis Joplin, Woodstock, 1969.

Taylor Mead for the photograph of himself. Photo: Raymond Foye, copyright © 1986, New York.

The Museum of Modern Art Film Stills Archive for the photograph of Ron Rice.

Michael Ochs Archives, Venice, California, for the photograph of George Martin.

The Music Division, New York Public Library, Lincoln Center, Astor, Lenox and Tilden Foundation, for the photograph of Country Joe MacDonald.

The Billy Rose Theater Collection, New York Public Library, Lincoln Center, Astor, Lenox and Tilden Foundation, for the photograph of Jean Cocteau, the photograph of Alexandro Jodorowsky, the photograph of John Howard Lawson, and the photograph of the Fillmore West.

Stereo Review for the photograph of Kris Kristofferson. Photo: Baron Wolman.

If any required acknowledgments have been omitted or any rights overlooked, it is unintentional and forgiveness is requested.

*Published by Alfred van der Marck Editions